Sports Science

40 Goal-Scoring, High-Flying, Medal-Winning Experiments for Kids

Jim Wiese

Illustrations by Ed Shems

John Wiley & Sons, Inc.

For Barbara

Published by John Wiley & Sons, Inc., New York
Published simultaneously in Canada

Design and Production by Navta Associates, Inc.

The publisher and the author have made every reasonable effort to ensure that the experiments and activities in this book are safe when conducted as instructed but assume no responsibility for any damage caused or sustained while performing the experiments or activities in the book. Parents, guardians, and/or teachers should supervise young readers who undertake the experiments and activities in this book.

Wiley also publishes its books in a variety of electronic formats. Some content that appears in print may not be available in electronic books. For more information about Wiley products, visit our web site at www.wiley.com.

Library of Congress Cataloging-in-Publication Data:

Wiese, Jim, date.
    Sports science : 40 goal-scoring, high-flying, medal-winning
experiments for kids / by Jim Wiese.
        p. cm.
Includes index.
    ISBN 0-471-44258-5 (pbk. : acid-free paper)
    1. Physics—Experiments. 2. Sports—Experiments. I. Title.
QC26 .W54 2002
530'.078—dc21   2002003461

Printed in the United States of America

10 9 8 7 6 5 4 3 2 1

Acknowledgments

I have always been interested in sports. I was not born a natural athlete but found that through hard work and practice I could improve in the sports I loved best—basketball, golf, and running. When I later entered college, I took several classes about the science of sports and learned that by applying scientific principles to my training, I could improve my skills even more. I even pursued graduate degrees in exercise physiology, wanting to do research for myself. Much of what you'll find in this book began in my own life, either as something I learned in one of my classes or in an article I read, or as something I wanted to study for myself. I hope that the activities in this book will get others to think about sports in a different way.

A lot of people have shared their interest in sports and sports science with me. I would especially like to thank Charley Sarver at Biola University, Dr. Ford Hess at Humboldt State Univerity, and Dr. Peter Lindsay at the University of Alberta for their dedication to sports and sports science, and for their ability to inspire others.

Again, I would like to thank the team of people at John Wiley who worked to make this book a reality. I would especially like to acknowledge the work of my editor, Kate Bradford. Her professionalism in every aspect of the publishing process always brings out the best in my writing.

Contents

Introduction

Have you ever watched a baseball game and asked yourself how the pitcher was able to make the ball curve? Or have you wondered how a figure skater can spin on one foot in such a way that she turns faster and faster? Or have you ever tried to figure out how to make your skateboard jump up off the ground? If you've ever thought about these and other questions, *Sports Science* is the place to find the answers. *Sports Science* lets you investigate the science behind many different sports, from baseball to biking to snowboarding to throwing a Frisbee. So get ready for over 40 exciting activities that will let you learn more about yourself and the sports you love.

How to Use This Book

This book starts with a chapter called Getting in the Zone, which talks about the most important part of your body in sports (your brain!). Then the rest of the chapters describe the science behind sports that use balls, blades, skis, and boards, rackets, wheels, and other things. In each chapter there are several projects on that topic. Each project includes a list of materials, a step-by-step procedure to follow, and an explanation of why the project turned out the way it did. Words in **bold** type are defined in the glossary at the back of the book. You'll be able to find most of the materials you need for these projects around the house or at your neighborhood hardware or grocery store. Some of the projects have a section called More Fun Stuff to Do that lets you try different variations on the original activity. Sections called Sports Science in Action give examples of how science is used by some well-known and some not-so-well-known sports figures.

Being a Good Scientist

- Read through the instructions once completely before you start the activity or experiment.

- Collect all the equipment you'll need before you start the activity or experiment.

- Keep a notebook in which you write down what you do in your experiment or project and what happens.

- Follow the instructions carefully. *Do not attempt to do by yourself any steps that require the help of an adult.*

- If your experiment or project does not work properly the first time, try again or try doing it in a slightly different way. In real life, experiments don't always work out perfectly the first time.

- Always have an open mind that asks questions and looks for answers. The basis of good science is asking good questions and finding the best answers.

Increasing Your Understanding

- Make small changes in the design of the equipment or project to see if the results stay the same. Change only one thing at a time so you can tell which change caused a particular result.

- Make up an experiment or activity to test your own ideas about how things work.

- Look at the things around you for examples of the scientific principles that you have learned.

- Don't worry if at first you don't understand the things around you. There are always new things to discover. Remember that many of the most famous discoveries were made by accident.

Using This Book to Do a Science Fair Project

Many of the activities in this book can serve as the starting point for a science fair project. After doing the experiment as it is written in the book, what questions come to mind? Some possible projects are suggested in the section of the activities called More Fun Stuff to Do.

To do a science fair project, you will have to follow the **scientific method.** When following the scientific method, you begin with a **hypothesis** (an educated guess about the results of an experiment you are going to perform), test it with an experiment, analyze the results, and draw a conclusion. For example, if you enjoyed the Think Fast activity, you may want to find out if boys or girls have a faster reaction time. A hypothesis for this experiment could be that girls have a faster reaction time than boys. Next you will have to devise an experiment to test your hypothesis. In the Think Fast example, you might test the reaction time for several of your friends. Make sure you test at least 5 other boys and 5 other girls. The more people you test, the more reliable your data is and the more accurate your conclusion. Next you will analyze the data you recorded. In the Think Fast example, you could create a table showing the sex of each person and his or her reaction time. You could also find the average reaction time for each group and compare those results. To find the average reaction time, add the reaction times in each group, then divide by the number of people in that group. Finally, you should come up with a conclusion that shows how your results prove or disprove your hypothesis.

A Word of Warning

Some science experiments can be dangerous. *Ask an adult to help you with experiments that call for adult help, such as those that involve matches, knives, or other sharp instruments.* Don't forget to ask your parents' permission to use household items, and put away your equipment and clean up your work area when you have finished experimenting. Good scientists are careful and avoid accidents.

Getting in the Zone

Starting Right

ou may not realize it, but your muscles are not the most important part of your body when you are doing a sport. Believe it or not, the most important part is your brain! The brain is part of your nervous system. The nervous system consists of your brain, spinal cord, and nerves. **Nerves** are special cells that communicate by using electrochemical impulses. An **electrochemical impulse** uses chemicals to send an electrical signal. So, the nervous system is an elaborate communication system that collects information and sends messages throughout your body. Your brain alone contains more than 100 billion nerve cells.

Sensory nerves collect information about your environment. They then change this information into sensations such as hot, cold, touch, pressure, and pain. They send this information to your brain, which then decides how to react. Once your brain decides on the appropriate response, it sends messages to other nerves called **motor nerves,** which direct your muscles to move.

The activities in this section will help you investigate how your brain and nervous system help you perform better in sports.

Project 1
THINK FAST

In many sports you need to react very quickly to something. For example, you may have to return a tennis ball that is moving at 60 miles (100 km) an hour or more or swing a bat at a baseball moving just as fast. You barely have time between when you first see the ball moving toward you and when you have to hit it back. In that short time your brain has to tell your body to move, and your body has to react. How long does it take? And can you improve your reaction time? Try this activity to find out.

Materials
ruler
helper

Procedure

1. Hold a ruler up vertically by the 12-inch (30-cm) end so that the 0-inch (0-cm) end is closest to the ground.

2. Have a helper stand facing you so that his thumb and index fingers of one hand are on either side of the bottom of the ruler. The thumb and index finger should be close to the ruler, but not touching it.

3. Drop the ruler at any time. With his hand held steady, your helper should try to catch the ruler as quickly as possible between his thumb and index finger.

4. Measure the distance the ruler fell before it was caught. Use the Reaction Time Table below to convert the distance the ruler falls into a time.

REACTION TIME TABLE

Distance	Time (seconds)
2 inches (5 cm)	0.101 seconds
4 inches (10 cm)	0.143 seconds
6 inches (15 cm)	0.175 seconds
8 inches (20 cm)	0.202 seconds
10 inches (25 cm)	0.226 seconds
12 inches (30 cm)	0.247 seconds

Explanation

The ruler will fall a short distance and your helper will catch it between his thumb and index finger. The distance the ruler falls can be used to determine your helper's reaction time. **Reaction time** is the amount of time it takes for a message to travel from the brain to the muscles in the body and cause a movement.

When the ruler drops, the motor cortex of the brain sends an electro-chemical message to the fingers. The **motor cortex** is the area of the brain responsible for creating and sending the messages that cause movement. The message travels along the thick bundles of nerve cells, the spinal cord, that are inside the bones of the spine. Then the message travels to the finger muscles through the smaller bundles of motor nerves that branch from the spinal cord. The finger muscles get the message and close, catching the ruler.

SPORTS SCIENCE IN ACTION

A good pitcher in the major leagues can throw a ball at speeds of between 90 and 100 miles per hour (144 and 160 km/h). What does that mean to a batter? The ball will take about 0.46 to 0.41 seconds to travel from a pitcher's hand to the plate. If you figure it takes about 0.3 seconds to actually swing, the batter may have only 0.1 to 0.2 seconds to decide when and where to swing and get the message to the arm and hand muscles. It's truly amazing that the human body can perform at this speed.

ON THE LEVEL

Your brain controls many functions in your body without your even having to think about them. For example, it keeps your lungs breathing in and out and makes your eyes blink. Your ability to balance or even just stand upright is also controlled by the brain. To learn more about how the brain does this, try this activity.

Materials

2-by-4-by-24-inch (5-by-10-by-60-cm) piece of wood (measurements do not have to be exact)

stopwatch or watch with a second hand

Procedure

1. Lay the board flat on the floor.

2. Step on the board with one foot near the middle of the board.

3. Lift your other foot off the ground and try to balance yourself on only one foot. Can you do it?

4. Continue to try to balance over a period of 5 minutes. Does your balance improve in that amount of time?

More Fun Stuff to Do

Get a longer piece of wood and lay it flat. Can you walk from one end of the board to the other without losing your balance and falling? Try practicing for several days. Do you get better at walking the length of the board?

Explanation

You should be able to learn to balance yourself on the board after several minutes.

Your sense of balance is controlled by parts of your inner ear. Small granules in two fluid-filled sacs detect which way is up and which way is down, and three fluid-filled semicircular canals detect motion.

SEMI CIRCULAR CANALS

COCHLEA
(USED IN HEARING)

INNER EAR

At the bottom of the sacs are sensory cells that contain small hair fibers. When you stand up, **gravity,** a force that pulls all objects toward Earth, pulls down on the granules. The granules touch the hair fibers, which sends a message to the brain and tells it that you are upright.

For example, when you lose your balance and begin to fall to the right, gravity pulls the granules to the right. The hair fibers then send a message to the brain

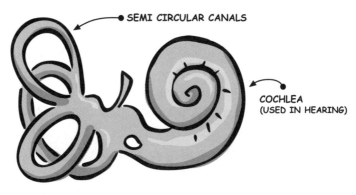

GRANULES

FLUID

HAIR CELLS

telling it that you are tilting to the right. The brain sends a message to the muscles in your neck and legs, trying to get your head and the rest of your body back in balance. With practice, you learn what kinds of little adjustments your body needs to make to balance. When you walk the length of a longer board you learn to balance by a similar process.

SPORTS SCIENCE IN ACTION

Balance is very important in the sport of women's gymnastics. The balance beam is a piece of wood that is 4 inches (10 cm) wide, 5.5 feet (1.67 m) off the ground, and 16 feet (4.85 m) long. In addition to balancing on the beam and walking from one end to the other, gymnasts have to perform flips, spins, and other maneuvers on the beam without losing their balance throughout the entire routine! It's a remarkable skill that takes a keen sense of balance and many years of practice.

Project 3
DREAMING OF GREATNESS

You've been practicing shooting free throws for several days and still don't seem to get any better. Is there anything else you can do to improve your shooting ability? Try this activity to find out.

Materials

basketball
basketball hoop
paper

pencil
2 helpers

Procedure

1. After warming up, you and your two helpers should each take 20 free throws at the basket. (If shooting from the free-throw line is too difficult, take your shots from somewhere closer to the basket.) Record the number of baskets each of you makes.

2. For the next week, you and your helpers should each do a different thing: one helper should not practice basketball at all; the other helper should shoot 10 free throws each day; and you should not practice with an actual basketball and hoop. Instead you should mentally shoot 10 free-throw shots each day. To mentally shoot free throws, close your eyes and picture yourself standing at the free-throw line, looking at the basket. Think about having the ball in your hand, doing any dribbles you might take before the shot, and finally making the shot itself. Picture yourself shooting the perfect shot and the ball going into the basket.

3. After the week is over, return to the basketball court and have everyone shoot another 20 free throws. Record each person's results and compare them to the number of shots made the previous week.

Explanation

After a week, both the helper who practiced by actually shooting the free throws and you, who practiced only by mentally shooting free throws, should make more free throws than the helper who didn't practice at all.

Mentally practicing free throws, or any other sports activity, is an important way to improve your performance. Mental rehearsal is believed to work in much the same way that physically repeating an activity does. Both mental and physical practice reinforce the messages that are sent from the brain to the muscles, coordinating the movement, so both lead to improved performance.

Mental rehearsal, sometimes called visualization, is used by most top-ranking athletes today. Gymnasts imagine doing a perfect routine on the uneven parallel bars, field goal kickers imagine a perfect kick that sends the football through the middle of the goal posts, and golfers imagine the swing and flight of the golf ball that lands perfectly on the green.

Although mental practicing can improve skills, you still need to physically practice to learn the skill in the first place and to build up your muscles as well. The coordinated message pattern from the brain to your muscles to perform a specific task needs to be in place first for the mental practicing to work.

SPORTS SCIENCE IN ACTION

In one study of visualization, scientists put electrodes on the muscles of a world-class skier to detect electrical activity. The skier was then asked to close his eyes and visualize each moment as he performed a perfect downhill race on a familiar ski slope. Bursts of muscular activity were recorded by the electrodes as the skier visualized hitting a jump or a rough part of the race. It was almost as if he were really skiing down the slope!

Project 4
CROSS OVER

Michael Jordan, the best basketball player in the world, once tried to play professional baseball. He turned out not to be that good at it. If Michael was such a good professional basketball player, why did he have trouble playing professional baseball? Try this activity to find out.

Materials

basketball   baseball
basketball hoop   bat
paper   helper
pencil

Procedure

1. Warm up by practicing shooting free throws with your helper at a basketball hoop. Then each of you should take 20 free throws. (If shooting from the free-throw line is too difficult, take your shots from somewhere closer to the basket.) Record the number of free throws you each make.

2. For the next week, you should each practice shooting 20 free throws each day.

3. After a week, return to the basketball hoop, and each shoot another 20 free throws. Record your results and compare them to the number of shots made the previous week. What happens?

4. Next, go to a field and each try to hit 20 baseballs. How does this activity compare to your free-throw ability?

More Fun Stuff to Do

Repeat the investigation using two other activities. For example, practice shooting free throws all week then try kicking a football. What effect does practicing one sport have on your ability to perform another?

Explanation

After a week's practice, you should improve the number of free throws that you make. However, your practice probably won't affect your ability to hit a baseball.

Although there are some activities, such as running and jumping, that are common to many sports, the ability to perform a specific task, such as shooting a basketball or hitting a baseball, is not easily transferred from one sport to another, especially when performing at the highest level. For example, most athletes will lift weights to make their muscles stronger and run or cycle to improve their heart and lungs. But each athlete will spend hours and hours performing their specific task, teaching the brain and muscles how to coordinate the movements in their event. Each time an athlete performs a task, such as shooting a basketball, the proper nerve path that carries the message to the muscles in the arm and hand, as well as the proper sequence of muscle contractions that produces a shot that goes in the basket, are reinforced. With repeated practice, the information for this basketball shot becomes imprinted in the memory of the brain and can be recalled the next time you want to make the same shot.

SPORTS SCIENCE IN ACTION

When Michael Jordan first retired from professional basketball, he was the greatest player in the world. He was a finely tuned athlete who had practiced basketball for years. After he retired, he wanted to become a professional baseball player, a sport that he had excelled at in high school. Although he learned to become a good fielder, he always had trouble with his batting. It wasn't that he didn't practice enough, it was just a matter of neurology (the study of how the brain and nerves works) and physiology (the study of how the body works). Michael had trained his brain, nerves, and muscles to perform in a certain way, to play basketball. When he tried to teach them to perform a new way, they just couldn't respond quickly enough. Michael went back to playing basketball, where his years of training paid off, and he again became the best player in the world!

After time, the athlete's body becomes trained to make that shot extremely well. If the athlete suddenly asks her body to do a different thing, the body won't respond as well. Whether you're a skateboarder learning to perform an "ollie" or an ice-skater learning a "triple axle," you have to practice the series of movements that allow you to perform each task. To perform at the highest level, you need to practice a lot!

Project 5
LEARNING NEW TRICKS

You have learned how to do a lot of sports activities in your life. When you were little, you learned how to run and how to throw a ball. Later on, maybe you learned how to swim and how to skateboard. What is the best way to learn how to play a new sport? Practice, practice, practice, of course. Try the next activity to learn more about how the brain learns new things, and why practice is important.

Materials

broom
2-by-12-by-24-inch (5-by-30-by-60 cm) piece of wood plank
stopwatch or watch with a second hand
helper

Procedure

1. Lay the broom flat on the floor.

2. Place the wooden plank on the handle of the broom so that the broom is near the center of the length of the plank.

3. Have your helper step on the plank so that one foot is placed near each end of the plank.

4. Time your helper for 5 minutes while she tries to learn to balance the plank on the broom handle so that neither end is touching the floor.

5. After your helper has had 5 minutes to learn to balance, it's your turn. You will also have 5 minutes to learn this new task, but you will spread your 5 minutes out over the day. Practice for 1 minute at a time, then stop for several hours. Your total practice time should be no more than 5 minutes.

6. The next day, both you and your helper should try to balance on the board. Who has learned to balance better?

Explanation

Even though you both had the same amount of practice time, because you spread out your practice over a longer period you learned to balance better than your helper, who tried to learn all at once.

Although no one is exactly sure how the brain learns, the most common theory is that it needs consolidation time to learn a new task well. **Consolidation time** is time when your brain stores the information about how to do a new task in a more permanent way. When you first learn a new task, whether it is how to balance on a board or how to do a new math problem, the information is stored temporarily as an electrical code within the brain. This electrical code is not stable, which means that you will quickly lose the information when you stop doing the task. However, if the task is practiced over a longer time, the electrical code is changed and stored in a more permanent, stable chemical code. Memory stored as a chemical is remembered better in the long term, so you perform the task better the next time you try it.

Flying High!

Ball Sports

Many sports involve throwing, kicking, or hitting balls. An outfielder in baseball throws a baseball toward home plate, a quarterback in football throws a football to a running receiver, and a soccer player kicks the soccer ball to a teammate.

When a ball is thrown, hit, or kicked, a force is put on it to cause it to move. A **force** is a push or pull. This force gives the ball speed. The speed of a ball will help determine how fast or how far it will move. But other forces act on balls as they move. Once a ball is thrown, hit, or kicked up in the air, gravity acts on it to bring it back to the ground. **Gravity** is the attraction between two objects due to their mass. As the ball moves through the air, the air creates resistance to the motion of a moving ball, which can cause the ball to slow down or change direction. Friction between a rolling ball and the ground also causes it to slow down.

To learn more about the way balls move and why different types of balls are used in different sports, try the activities in this chapter.

Project 1
THROW IT HIGHER

There are many sports that involve throwing a ball into the air. How high can you throw a tennis ball into the air? And how would you measure your throw? Try this activity to find out.

Materials

tennis ball   paper
stopwatch   friend
pencil

Note: This activity should be done in an outdoor area, away from trees, houses, and other people.

Procedure

1. Have your friend be the timer and you be the thrower.

2. Throw the ball straight up, as high as you can as your friend times how long the ball is in the air. The timer should start the

stopwatch the instant the ball
leaves your hand and stop it the
instant the ball hits the ground.
Record your time in seconds on a
piece of paper.

3. Repeat the
experiment
several
times. Use
the longest
time the ball
was in the air
to make the
following
calculations:

a. Since the time you measured involves both the time the ball
goes up and the time it comes down, divide your time by
two. You only need the time the ball was moving upward.

b. Next, square the time you calculated in step 3a (multiply it
by itself).

c. Then multiply the result of step 3b by 16 for the height your
ball went in feet or by 4.9 for the height of your throw in
meters.

Explanation

In this activity you threw a ball into the air and calculated the
approximate height you were able to throw it. For example, if the
ball was in the air for 3.2 seconds, you would calculate the height
the ball reached this way: (a) time the ball took to go up and down,
which is 3.2 seconds, divided by 2 to get 1.6 seconds; (b) square the
time you got in step a ($1.6 \times 1.6 = 2.56$); and (c) multiply the result
by 16 (or 4.9) to get the approximate height the ball reached—
$2.56 \times 16 = 41$ feet or $2.56 \times 4.9 = 12.5$ meters.

When you throw a ball into the air, gravity acts to pull it back to
Earth. Gravity causes objects to decelerate (move slower) when they
move away from Earth and to accelerate (move faster) when they
move toward Earth. You throw the ball upward with a certain speed.
Gravity begins to slow the ball down until it eventually stops the
ball's upward motion at the instant it reaches the highest point of the

throw. Gravity then causes the ball to move back toward the ground. The ball moves faster the longer it falls. Because it moves faster as it falls, the ball falls farther for each second. The mathematical relationship between the distance the ball travels and the time the ball falls is $d = (\frac{1}{2}a) \times t^2$ (distance the object falls equals one-half the acceleration due to gravity times the time the object falls squared), which is the formula you used in this activity.

The faster you throw a ball, the higher it goes and the longer it takes gravity to pull it back to the ground.

SPORTS SCIENCE IN ACTION

Not all throwing sports use balls. In the summer Olympics, there are four throwing events—the javelin, discus, shot put, and hammer. In Britain, there is even a sport that involves the throwing of a well-known brand of rubber boot, size 8. The current men's record for throwing this rubber boot is 173 feet (52.3 m)!

Project 2
THROW IT FARTHER

The outfielder wants to throw the baseball to home plate, the soccer goalie wants to kick the soccer ball past midfield, and the basketball player wants to shoot a shot from the center of the court. How can each of these athletes get the ball to go as far as possible? Try this activity to find out.

Materials

garden hose attached to an outside faucet

Procedure

1. Turn the water on full force.

2. Point the hose so that it is horizontal to the ground. Note how far the water travels.

3. Gradually point the end of the hose higher and note how far the water goes. At what angle does the water travel the farthest?

Explanation

As you increase the angle of the hose, the water will begin to travel a greater distance. After the hose reaches a certain angle, however, the water will begin to travel a shorter distance. The water should travel the farthest when it comes out of the hose at about a 45-degree angle.

When a ball is thrown at an angle, two components make up the motion of the object. There is a vertical component, which causes the ball to move up and down, and a horizontal component, which causes it to move forward. The vertical component of the ball's motion changes because of gravity, but the horizontal component remains constant throughout the ball's flight.

If a ball is thrown at a high angle, it has a large vertical component, which will make it stay in the air longer. However, it will have a small horizontal component, so it will not travel as far. If a ball is thrown at a low angle, it will have a large horizontal component but a small vertical component. That means that the ball will only stay

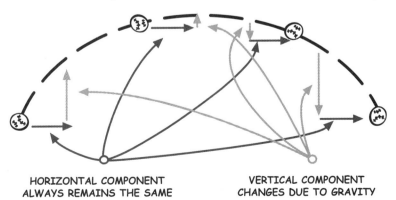

HORIZONTAL COMPONENT
ALWAYS REMAINS THE SAME

VERTICAL COMPONENT
CHANGES DUE TO GRAVITY

in the air a short time. To get a ball to travel farther, you need to trade off time in the air (vertical component) for speed of the ball (horizontal component). This is usually at about a 45-degree angle.

Nevertheless, not every throw should be at 45 degrees. There are several other factors that influence the best angle to throw for distance. For example, if air resistance is a factor, such as on a windy day, you should throw the ball lower. Also, because of the way your body works, you can throw with a greater force when you throw at a lower angle.

SPORTS SCIENCE IN ACTION

All balls, whether thrown or hit, fall back to the Earth's surface because of gravity. But what if you hit a ball somewhere off of Earth, like on the surface of the moon? In 1971, Alan Shepard traveled to the moon as part of the Apollo space program. As an experiment, he took with him a golf club and several golf balls. When he hit a golf ball on the moon, he discovered, as expected, that it traveled much farther than on Earth due to the moon's lower pull of gravity. But the ball still eventually curved back to the surface. Those balls are still sitting on the moon's surface.

Project 3
CURVEBALL

Many scientists have argued whether a thrown baseball can actually be made to curve in a certain direction as it moves toward home plate. As a baseball travels through the air, the air will flow around the ball. It is in the motion of the air around the ball where interesting things can happen. Try this activity to learn more.

Materials

strip of paper 1 by 12 inches (2.5 by 30 cm)

Procedure

1. Hold the strip of paper just below your lower lip.

2. Blow hard across the top surface.

3. Observe what happens.

More Fun Stuff to Do

Draw diagonal lines joining opposite corners of a 3-by-5-inch (7.5-by-12.5-cm) index card. Push a thumbtack through the center of the card at the point where the diagonal lines meet. Hold the card under a thread spool so that the thumbtack point is in the opening of the spool hole. (Do not push the thumbtack into the spool.) Lift the card and the spool to your mouth. Blow hard down the hole opposite the card while you slowly take your hand off the card. Can you blow the card off the spool?

Explanation

When you blow across the top surface of the paper strip, the strip will rise. In the More Fun Stuff to Do experiment, when you blow through the spool hole, the card will stick to the spool instead of blowing off.

These are both examples of Bernoulli's principle, named for the Swiss scientist Daniel Bernoulli. **Bernoulli's principle** says that as air moves faster it will produce a lower air pressure. When you blow along the top of the paper, the air on the top of the paper starts moving faster than the air on the bottom. This creates an area of lower air pressure above the paper than below the paper. The higher air pressure below the paper pushes up and causes the paper to rise.

So what does this activity have to do with a curveball? Plenty! When a pitcher throws a ball with a lot of spin, part of the spin is in the direction of the air flow and part of the spin is in the opposite direction of the air flow. On the side where the spin and the air flow are in the same direction, the result is an increase in the speed of the air over that side of the ball. Just as in this experiment, the increased speed leads to a small decrease in air pressure on that side of the ball, so the ball moves in that direction, pushed by the higher pressure on the other side of the ball. As the ball continues to spin on its flight to the plate, it curves from its normal path.

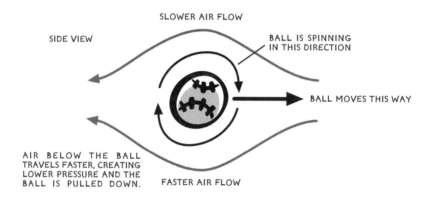

SLOWER AIR FLOW

SIDE VIEW

BALL IS SPINNING
IN THIS DIRECTION

BALL MOVES THIS WAY

AIR BELOW THE BALL
TRAVELS FASTER, CREATING
LOWER PRESSURE AND THE
BALL IS PULLED DOWN.

FASTER AIR FLOW

SPORTS SCIENCE IN ACTION

Another sport where ball spin is important is tennis. With a proper hit, a tennis player can put what is called topspin on a tennis ball. With topspin, the air on the top side of the ball moves in the same direction that the ball is traveling while the bottom side of the ball moves in the opposite direction. This means the air moving above the ball will have a lower velocity and a higher air pressure while the air moving below the ball will have a higher velocity and a lower air pressure. This air pressure imbalance creates what is known as the Magnus effect, and the ball moves downward more than it normally would.

STABLE SPIN

In the last activity you saw how spinning a baseball can make it curve a certain way. Are there any other reasons for spinning a ball? Try this activity to find out.

Materials

sheet of paper   clean plastic lid, such as one from
pencil   a cottage cheese container
nail   ruler

Procedure

1. Place the sheet of paper on a table.

2. Hold the pencil upright with its point on the paper. Let go of the pencil. What happens?

3. Use the nail to make a small hole in the center of the plastic lid. Push the pencil through the hole so that the pencil point is about 1 inch (2.5 cm) from the lid.

4. Hold the pencil and lid upright with the pencil point on the paper. Let go of the pencil. What happens?

5. Hold the pencil and lid upright between your palms with the pencil point on the paper. Move your palms in opposite directions then release the pencil to make it spin on its point. What happens to the spinning pencil?

Explanation

When you first try to stand the pencil on its point, it falls over due to the pull of gravity. It also falls over with the cottage cheese lid attached. However, when you spin the pencil with the cottage cheese lid attached, it balances on its point.

A spinning object is more stable than an object that doesn't spin, because the spinning of an object creates what is called angular momentum. The **law of angular momentum** says that a rotating object will stay rotating in that same way unless acted on by an outside force. Angular momentum, and therefore stability, increase with the mass and diameter of the object. Adding the plastic cottage cheese lid increases stability, making it easier for a pencil to spin on its point.

Friction and gravity eventually stop the pencil and plastic lid from spinning. Friction between the pencil and paper slows it down, while gravity causes it to tip over.

A baseball that spins has a more stable flight path than one that doesn't spin. When the pitcher throws a spinning baseball toward home plate, its angular momentum causes is to fly in a straighter line than a thrown baseball without spin.

Another ball that should spin when it is thrown is a football. This is called throwing a "spiral." Because of the angular momentum, a spinning football will be more stable in its flight. That means the receiver (the person who has to catch the football) will be better able to predict where the football will land and can run there and catch it.

Project 5
DIMPLES

Have you ever looked at the dimples (small impressions) in a golf ball and wondered why they are there? Try this next activity to learn what dimples do to the golf ball's flight.

Materials

smooth plastic ball (a ball-hockey ball works best)
plastic Wiffle ball
helper

Note: This activity should be done outside in an open area on a day without much wind.

Procedure

1. Stand about 5 yards (5 m) from your helper.

2. Throw the smooth plastic ball between you and your helper. Note the flight of the ball on the throws.

3. Slowly increase the distance between you and your helper as you throw the ball back and forth until you reach the maximum distance you can throw the ball. Continue to note the flight of the ball on the throws. Mark the distance that you can throw the smooth plastic ball.

4. Return to standing 5 yards (5 m) from your helper and repeat playing catch, but this time do it with the plastic Wiffle ball. How is its flight path different from that of the smooth plastic ball? Which ball can you throw farther?

More Fun Stuff to Do

Try hitting different golf balls at a practice golf range using the same golf club. Practice hitting both older balls that have worn their dimples smooth and newer balls that have deeper holes. Which balls can you hit farther?

Explanation

When you throw a smooth plastic ball, it will take a straight and fairly regular flight. The Wiffle ball, in contrast, will usually rise higher in the air and will often curve to the left or right. The ball that can be thrown farthest depends on a number of factors, but the Wiffle ball will often go farther than the smooth plastic ball. In the More Fun Stuff to Do activity, you should be able to hit a newer golf ball with deeper dimples farther than the old golf ball with worn dimples.

The dimples on a golf ball change the flight of the ball by changing the way that it moves through the air. The air resistance on a golf ball comes from two factors: the pressure difference between the front and back of the ball and the friction between the surface of the ball and the air. With a smooth ball, there is less friction between the ball and the air so the air flows smoothly around the ball. This creates vortices, areas of swirling air, behind the ball. In these vortices behind the ball, the air has lower pressure than in front of the ball, so the ball slows down. With a dimpled ball, there is more friction between the surface and the ball. This friction holds the air closer to the ball and disrupts the formation of the vortices behind the ball. So the dimpled ball slows down less than the smooth ball and can travel farther.

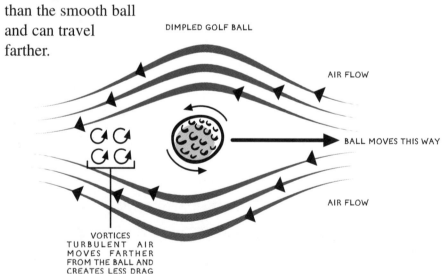

DIMPLED GOLF BALL

AIR FLOW

BALL MOVES THIS WAY

AIR FLOW

VORTICES
TURBULENT AIR
MOVES FARTHER
FROM THE BALL AND
CREATES LESS DRAG

The flight of the golf ball or Wiffle ball is also affected by Bernoulli's principle. A golf ball hit by a golf club should have backspin. With backspin, as the spinning golf ball travels through the air, the air on top of the ball is moving in the direction of the air flow, while air on the bottom of the ball is moving in the opposite direction of the air flow. As described earlier in Curveball, because of Bernoulli's principle, the spinning ball will move up, pushed by the higher pressure of the air on the bottom of the ball. If the hitter makes a mistake and hits the golf ball with side spin, this same effect will cause the ball to curve dramatically to the left (a hook for a right-handed player) or right (a slice for a right-handed player).

Besides the dimple patterns, the materials that make up both the cover and elastic core of the golf ball will affect the distance the golf ball will travel. To learn more about this, try Follow the Bouncing Ball.

Project 6
HEADING RIGHT

In soccer you sometimes have to use your head to hit the ball. But if you aim the ball directly into the net, it may go wide. To learn why, try this activity.

Materials

piece of paper

pencil

ruler

books

rubber ball

protractor

2-by-4-by-12-inch (5-by-10-by-30-cm) piece of wood

Procedure

1. Place the paper on a table. Use the ruler and pencil to draw a horizontal line that divides the paper's length approximately in half.

2. Use the ruler and pencil to draw a line on the 4-inch (10-cm) side of the piece of wood that divides the length approximately in half.

3. Place the wood along the edge of the paper so that the lines meet. Make a mark on the paper where the lines meet.

4. Place several books behind the wood to hold it in place.

5. Use the pencil to place a small mark near one corner of the paper.

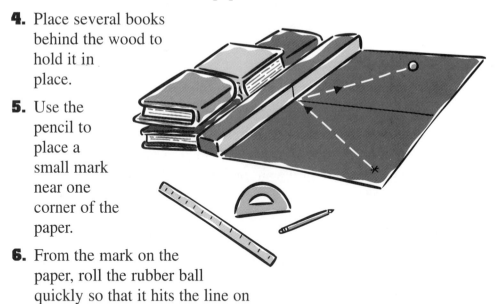

6. From the mark on the paper, roll the rubber ball quickly so that it hits the line on the board.

7. Note the direction the ball rolls after it hits the board and place a mark on the paper at a point over which the ball rolled.

8. Draw a line from the first mark on the paper to the point where the board met the paper.

9. Draw a line from the point where the board met the paper to the second mark.

10. Use the protractor to measure the angles between each of the lines you just drew and the original line on the paper. What do you notice?

More Fun Stuff to Do

Try this activity several more times but start the ball from different points so that the ball rolls at different angles when it bounces off the board. What do you notice?

Explanation

The angle that the ball made when it rolled toward the board should be equal to the angle that it makes after it bounces off the board. If you try different angles, such as in the More Fun Stuff to Do activity, the ball will still bounce off the board at the same angle that it goes toward the board.

When a moving object bounces off another object, the **angle of incidence,** the angle that the ball makes when it strikes the board, will equal the **angle of reflection,** the angle the ball makes after it bounces off the board. These angles are always measures off a line, called the normal line, which is perpendicular to the reflecting surface.

In soccer, when a ball bounces off your head, or any other part of your body, your body acts like the board, and the angle of incidence will equal the angle of reflection. By moving your head or other part of your body, you can change the direction of the angle of reflection. For example, if a ball is kicked toward your chest and you stand straight up, the ball will hit your chest and bounce away. But if you bend forward at the waist,

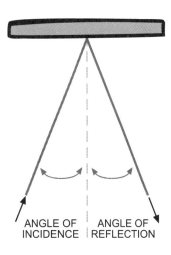

ANGLE OF INCIDENCE ANGLE OF REFLECTION

when the ball hits your chest, it will bounce down to your feet, where you can kick it to another team member.

SPORTS SCIENCE IN ACTION

When you kick a soccer ball, the ball will often move in different ways because of variations in your kick. So when Carnegie Mellon University was contracted by a large sports shoe company to test newly designed soccer shoes and soccer balls, they had to create a robot that would kick a soccer ball exactly the same every time. The robot leg was designed to approximate as close as possible the movements of the human leg. So when new soccer shoes let you kick a ball straighter, it may be because they were first tested by a robot!

Project 7
SOFT BOUNCE

In the previous activity you learned that a soccer ball bounces when it hits your body. But what if you don't want the ball to bounce? Try this activity to find out.

Materials

several balloons filled with water
helper

Note: This activity should be done in a large open area outside. You may also get wet performing this activity!

Procedure

1. Hold one water balloon and stand about 6 feet (2 m) away from your helper.

2. Have your helper stand with her arms held out stiffly in front of her.

3. Lob the water balloon to your helper. She should try to catch the water balloon without moving her hands toward her body. What happens?

4. If the water balloon doesn't break, each of you should take a step backward. Then the helper should lob the water balloon back to you. You should also try to catch the water balloon without moving your hands toward your body.

5. If the water balloon still hasn't burst, continue lobbing the water balloon back and forth, moving back a step each time, until it does. How far can you move without breaking the water balloon?

6. Repeat the activity with a new water balloon, but this time try catching the water balloon by moving your hands toward your body each time you catch it. How far can you go without breaking the water balloon if you try catching it this way?

More Fun Stuff to Do

Try stopping a fast-rolling soccer ball but keep your foot stiff. Next try stopping a fast-rolling soccer ball but this time move your foot slightly in the direction that the ball is moving as you stop the ball. Which way stops the ball so that it is closest to you?

Explanation

You will be able to more easily catch the water balloon without having it break when you move your hands toward your body as you catch the balloon. In the More Fun Stuff to Do, it will be easier to get the ball to stop closer to you if you move your foot slightly in the direction that the ball is moving.

In order to stop a moving object, such as a ball, you have to take away its momentum. You can do this by putting an impulse on the ball, equal to the momentum but in the opposite direction. An **impulse** is a force put on an object for a length of time. When you catch a water balloon, you have to take away its momentum. If you try to catch it with your hands held stiffly in front of you, the impulse has only a short time to act, so it uses a greater force and the water balloon breaks. But if you move your hands toward your body when you catch the water balloon, the impulse has a longer time to act and uses less force, so the water balloon doesn't break.

Impulse is also at work in soccer. When you want to stop a soccer ball that is moving toward you, you should move backward slightly to decrease the force necessary to stop the ball.

SPORTS SCIENCE IN ACTION

Pelé is one of the greatest soccer players ever. He could stop a speeding ball dead at his feet. It was as if his rock-hard body could instantly change into a big, soft cushion. Pelé knew that the secret to good ball control in soccer was to treat the ball as if it were something fragile, like an egg. As the ball moved quickly toward him, he would relax the part of his body that was going to hit the ball—his head, his chest, or his feet. By relaxing, he softened, or cushioned, the ball's impact, leaving the ball magically at his feet.

Project 8
FOLLOW THE BOUNCING BALL

You may have noticed that not all balls are the same. Can you imagine playing tennis with a baseball? The kind of ball you use in each sport is very important. One characteristic of a ball is how much it bounces. Try the next activity to learn more about the bounce in a ball.

Materials

smooth cement sidewalk
yardstick (meterstick)
tennis ball
paper

pencil
baseball
basketball
calculator

Procedure

1. Find a level area on a smooth cement sidewalk.

2. Hold the yardstick (meterstick) vertically in front of you with one hand. Place the 0 end of the yardstick (meterstick) on the ground.

3. Hold the tennis ball in the other hand so that the bottom of the ball is level with the top of the yardstick (meterstick).

4. Release the tennis ball, letting it bounce off the cement and up again. Note the maximum height the bottom of the tennis ball reaches with the bounce. Write the height on a piece of paper.

5. Repeat steps 3 and 4 using first the baseball, then the basketball.

6. Use the calculator to divide the maximum height each ball bounced by the height the ball started at, then multiply the answer by 100 percent. For example, if the tennis ball started at the top of the yardstick (meterstick),

it started at 36 inches (or 100 cm for the meterstick). If it then bounced to a maximum height of 18 inches (or 50 cm for the meterstick), the result would be:

$$18/36 = .50 \times 100\% = 50\%$$
$$50/100 = .50 \times 100\% = 50\%$$

More Fun Stuff to Do

Take a second tennis ball and put it into the freezer overnight. The next day, do the experiment again with the frozen ball and the regular ball to compare the heights that they bounce to. What do you find out?

Explanation

In this activity, the basketball should bounce back with the highest percentage, and the baseball should bounce back with the lowest percentage. The tennis ball should be in between the values of the other two. An average basketball will bounce to about 56 percent of its original height, a tennis ball will bounce to about 50 percent of its original height, and a baseball will bounce to only 32 percent of its original height. In the More Fun Stuff to Do activity, the frozen tennis ball should bounce much less than a normal ball.

When a ball rests in your hand, it is said to have **gravitational potential energy** (because of its position and the force of Earth's gravity). When you release the ball and the ball falls toward Earth, its potential energy is converted into **kinetic energy,** the energy of motion. When the ball hits the floor and stops, this kinetic energy is changed into another form of potential energy called elastic energy. **Elastic energy** is potential energy stored in an object when its shape is changed by stretching (pulling apart) or compressing (pushing together). The kinetic energy is transformed as the shape of the ball is deformed from its original round shape to a squashed shape. When the ball goes into this shape, the molecules that make it up are stretched apart in some places and squeezed together in others. What these molecules do next depends on the ball.

In some balls, such as a basketball, the molecules in the ball return to their original shape, and their elastic potential energy changes back into kinetic energy, which causes the ball to bounce up very high. In other balls, such as a baseball, some of the kinetic energy is changed into **thermal energy** (heat energy) by internal frictional forces in the ball and ground. This energy cannot be later converted to kinetic energy, the molecules in the ball do not return to their original shape, and the ball doesn't bounce very high.

When a ball is frozen, the molecules cannot quickly return to their original shape, so the frozen tennis ball does not bounce as high as a normal tennis ball.

The surface that a ball bounces against also affects the bounce. See the difference when you try bouncing the basketball on grass instead of on pavement.

SPORTS SCIENCE IN ACTION

Both golf balls and golf clubs must meet certain standards before they are allowed to be used in golf tournaments. The amount of bounce that a golf ball gets off a swung golf club, for example, has been set by the USGA at a maximum of 81 percent. Recently, the Callaway golf club manufacturing company designed a driver (the golf club that is used to hit the ball off a tee) that increases the amount of bounce to over 81 percent. Because this value exceeds the maximum value set by the USGA, the club cannot be used in golf tournaments in the United States. The club can, however, be used in golf tournaments in Europe and elsewhere around the world as well as by amateurs everywhere.

In recent years, home run hitters such as Mark McGwire, Barry Bonds, and Sammy Sosa seem to be hitting balls farther than in previous years. Some people suggested that this happened because baseballs have more bounce than they used to. The amount a baseball should bounce is between 51 and 57 percent when hit by a baseball bat swung at 60 mph (96 km/h). Because of this variety, different baseballs will "bounce" off a swung bat differently. If a batter can hit a baseball that has a 51 percent bounce 400 feet (121 m), then the same swing would send a baseball that has a 57 percent bounce almost 450 feet (136 m). Scientists checked hundreds of baseballs and found that they were in the normal bounce range. Maybe the batters were just getting better!

Project 9
FUZZ BALL

Have you ever wondered if the fuzz covering a tennis ball has a purpose or if it is just there to make the ball look better? To learn about the purpose of tennis ball fuzz try this activity.

Materials

smooth plastic ball the size of a tennis ball
plastic tub
measuring cup
water
new tennis ball

Procedure

1. Hold the plastic ball with your thumb and index finger on the sides of the ball. Hold the ball over the plastic tub.

2. Slowly pour 1 cup (250 ml) of water on the top of the ball. Notice how the water runs over the surface of the ball.

3. Hold the tennis ball with your thumb and index finger on the sides of the ball. Again hold the ball over the plastic tub.

4. Slowly pour 1 cup (250 ml) of water on the top of the ball. How does the water run over the surface of the tennis ball?

Explanation

The water will flow faster along the surface of the smooth plastic ball and more slowly along the surface of the fuzzy tennis ball.

Friction is resistance to motion between two objects that rub against each other. We often think of friction as occurring between two solid objects, such as between a car's tires and the road. But there is also friction between a liquid and a solid, such as in water moving on the surface of a plastic ball, and between air and a solid, such as when a tennis ball moves through the air. Friction depends on the roughness of the surface. The rougher the surface, the more friction. In this activity, the fuzzy tennis ball's surface is quite rough compared to that of the smooth plastic ball. Because the fuzzy surface creates more friction, the water will move more slowly over it.

What effect does the fuzz on a tennis ball have as it travels from the player who serves the ball to the player who receives it? Plenty! The friction from both the air and the surface of the court slow the ball down quite a bit. For example, if you see a professional tennis serve that leaves the racket at 125 mph (200 km/h), it will slow to about 81 mph (130 km/h) just before it bounces, 63 mph (100 km/h) after it bounces, and will arrive at the other player traveling at about 50 mph (80 km/h).

The fuzz on the tennis ball also causes the ball to react differently when it hits the playing surface. Tennis is usually played on a hard and relatively smooth surface. Tennis balls have fuzz on them to help the ball grip the surface better. This causes the ball to bounce rather than skid when it hits. The fuzz friction also increases the ability of a tennis player to direct the ball where she wants to hit it and to put spin on it.

SPORTS SCIENCE IN ACTION

The International Tennis Federation gives out the rules for the size, weight, and construction of tennis balls. Tennis balls are to be covered with either wool or synthetic felt. But there are differences among types of tennis balls. Tennis is played on different surfaces, such as clay, grass, asphalt, or another synthetic material. Different kinds of tennis balls are designed especially for each surface.

Project 10
THE BIG MO

Did you know that when you hit a pool ball with a cue stick, you are demonstrating the transfer of momentum? Try this activity to see one way in which science is involved with the game of pool.

Materials

plastic ruler with a groove down its length
several marbles all the same size

Procedure

1. Place the ruler flat on the table with the groove facing up.

2. Place one marble in the ruler's groove near one end. Give the marble a push and note its motion.

3. Place the marble back near the end of the groove. Place another marble in the groove near the center of the ruler.

4. Again give the marble near the end a push. What happens when the two marbles collide?

5. Place the first marble back near the end of the groove. This time place two marbles so they are touching each other near the center of the ruler.

6. Give the marble near the end a push. What happens when the marble collides with the two marbles near the center?

More Fun Stuff to Do

Try adding more marbles near the center of the ruler. What happens when they are hit by the moving marble?

Explanation

When the single marble rolls down the groove, it will roll at a constant speed. But when the marble rolls and strikes another marble, the first marble will stop, or slow down, and the marble that was originally stationary will begin to roll at the same speed as the first marble. When there are two marbles to hit, the first marble will again stop, but only the marble on the end farthest from the impact will begin to roll, again at the same speed as the first marble. If you place several marbles in a row, as in the More Fun Stuff to Do activity, the first marble will stop upon colliding with the marbles and only the marble on the end farthest from the impact will begin to roll, again at the same speed as the first marble.

The collision between the marbles shows the **law of conservation of momentum,** which says that the momentum of an object, or group of objects, will stay the same unless acted on by an outside force. The momentum of an object depends on both its mass and its speed (momentum = mass × speed). When the first marble rolls down the ruler's groove, it has a specific amount of momentum. This momentum remains the same because there is no force acting on the marble, so the marble rolls at a constant speed. (Actually there is a little friction working to slow the marble's rolling, but given a good push the friction will have only a small effect.) The second marble you put in the groove has no momentum because it is stationary. When the first marble collides with the stationary marble, the first marble transfers its momentum to the stationary marble and comes to rest. The marble that was previously at rest now has all the momentum. Because it has the same mass (and now the same momentum) as the first marble, it rolls off at the same speed as the first marble. When several stationary marbles are added in row, the momentum of the rolling marble is transferred through all the marbles until it reaches the end marble, which again begins to roll at the same speed as the first marble. However, once the marble begins to roll, friction begins to slow its speed.

This is what happens in pool when the cue ball hits a stationary numbered ball straight on (not at an angle). The cue ball will stop, transferring its momentum to the second ball, and the second ball will begin to roll with the same speed as the cue ball.

SPORTS SCIENCE IN ACTION

If the cue ball does not hit the stationary ball straight on, but instead strikes it at an angle, only part of the momentum is transferred from the cue ball to the second ball. The cue ball will bounce off the second ball at an angle and will continue to roll, while the second ball will also begin to roll. This kind of collision is an elastic collision. In an **elastic collision,** momentum is conserved as well as kinetic energy. *Conserved* means it isn't increased or decreased. While momentum is related to the speed of an object, kinetic energy is related to the speed of the object squared (speed multiplied by speed). When a cue ball strikes a stationary ball at an angle and kinetic energy is conserved the Pythagorean theorem takes over. The **Pythagorean theorem** says that in a right triangle, the square of the triangle's hypotenuse (the longest side) is equal to the sum of the squares of the other two sides. Since an elastic energy collision involves a squared value (speed), the paths the moving balls take after they collide will be at right angles to each other and will form part of a right triangle!

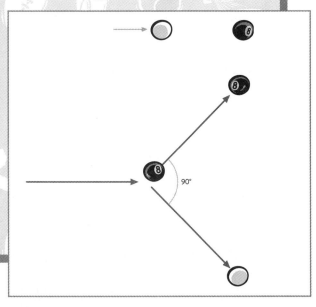

3 Slipping and Sliding

Blade, Ski, and Board Sports

Not every sport is done in the comfort of a heated sports arena or in the summer's warmth. Winter sports such as skiing, snowboarding, and ice-skating involve many areas of science, including balance, angular momentum, and friction.

Balance keeps the body upright and stable. It is easiest to keep a body in balance if its **center of gravity** is over the base of support that holds it up. The center of gravity of an object is the point where the effect of gravity on the object seems to be concentrated. When skiers, snowboarders, and skaters bend their knees and move their feet farther apart, they lower their center of gravity, increase the size of their base of support, and increase their balance and stability.

The law of angular momentum is the tendency of spinning objects to keep spinning unless acted on by an outside force. A skater spinning on the ice will keep spinning unless she puts her foot out to stop herself or friction eventually slows her down.

In some sports activities, such as ice-skating, downhill skiing, or tobogganing, you want to decrease the friction so that you will go faster. In other activities, such as cross-country skiing, you need low friction to move down hills, but you want some friction so that your skies will grip the snowy surface when you want to go uphill.

To learn more about the science behind blade, ski, and board sports, check out the activities in this chapter.

Project I
SKATING ON THIN ICE

On a cold winter day you go to the ice rink to skate. You lace up your skates, push off, and immediately slip and fall on the icy surface. Why, you wonder, do skates need to have thin, sharp metal blades? Try this activity to find out.

Materials

dish towel
ice cube
butter knife

Procedure

1. Fold the dish towel several times, then lay it on a flat surface such as a kitchen table.

2. Place the ice cube in the center of the towel.

3. Hold the knife blade with its wide flat side against the ice cube. Push down on the blade as hard as you can and hold it there for 30 seconds.

4. Lift the knife and look at the ice cube's surface. What do you see?

5. Hold the knife blade against the ice cube, this time with its cutting edge against the ice, and press down as hard as you can for 30 seconds.

6. Lift the knife and look at the ice cube's surface. What do you see this time?

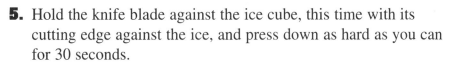

More Fun Stuff to Do

Connect two weights, such as heavy rocks, to opposite ends of a piece of thin copper wire that is 18 inches (45 cm) long. Place a large piece of ice on top of several stacked pieces of wood. Place the wire on top of the ice so that the weights hang suspended on either side of the ice. Observe the ice after 15 minutes. What has happened?

Explanation

The flat side of the knife will have no effect on the ice cube, while the sharp edge will make a narrow groove in the ice. In the More Fun Stuff to Do section, the wire will begin to cut through the ice.

While you exert the same force on the knife whether it is flat or on edge, you exert different amounts of pressure. **Pressure** is the amount of force divided by the area of the force. Because the area of the knife edge is less, while the force remains the same, the result is that you exert more pressure. Ice melts when it is placed under high pressure so in the area right below the knife edge, the solid ice turns to liquid water and the knife begins to make a groove in the cube. The higher the pressure, the more the ice melts.

This is the same thing that happens with ice skates. When you stand on the sharp skate blades of ice skates, the blades create high pressure on the ice and the ice melts below the blade. Why is it important? Because you actually skate on a thin layer of water. This layer of water creates less friction between your skates and the ice, so you move more easily. Friction between the skate blades and the ice also creates heat, which also helps melt the ice. Once the skate blade moves off of that particular area of ice, the ice surface quickly refreezes.

SPORTS SCIENCE IN ACTION

The sport of curling was recently added to the winter Olympics. Curling is sort of like playing marbles with big rocks on ice. One curler throws a large smooth granite stone so that it slides from one end of an ice surface toward a target at the other end. Near the target area, other curlers use brooms to sweep the ice surface in front of the stones. This isn't because the ice surface is dirty. When the players sweep the surface of the ice, the friction created by the moving bristles of the brooms melts some of the, ice producing a thin layer of water on the surface of the ice. This lets the rock travel straighter and farther. Sweeping the ice can also change the direction the stone is going. If the sweeping stops, the rock begins to slow down more rapidly.

SPEEDY SPIN

Have you ever watched an ice-skater spin on the ice? She starts spinning slowly, then seems to spin faster and faster without any additional pushes. How is this possible? Try this activity to find out.

Materials

swivel chair
2 heavy objects, such as hand weights or large books
helper

Procedure

1. Place the chair in the center of the room. Make sure you have enough space to turn in circles without stopping.

2. Sit in the chair, holding the two heavy objects in your lap. With your feet off the ground, have your helper push the chair so that it spins. Once your helper has pushed once, he should not touch the chair again. What happens as you spin?

3. Repeat step 2, except this time hold a heavy object in each hand. Start by holding the objects near your body. Have your helper spin the chair. As you spin, slowly move the objects outward until your arms are extended. What happens as you spin this time?

4. Repeat step 2 again, this time starting with the objects held away from your body with your arms extended. Have your helper spin the chair. As you spin, slowly move the objects inward until they are next to your body. What happens as you spin this time?

More Fun Stuff to Do

Watch an ice-skating competition on television. What do the performers do with their arms when they want to spin faster? What do they do with their arms when they want to spin slower?

Explanation

When your friend spun you on the chair the first time, you gradually slowed down and came to a stop. When you moved the heavy objects away from your body by extending your arms while spinning, your spin slowed down more quickly. When you then pulled in your arms and held the heavy objects close to your body while spinning, your spin sped up slightly.

Anything that rotates, whether it is a wheel rolling down a hill or a skater spinning on ice, keeps rotating until something stops it. This is called the law of angular momentum. Angular momentum equals

SPORTS SCIENCE IN ACTION

A human body can rotate in several ways, and there are many examples in sports, such as diving and gymnastics, where athletes use the law of angular momentum to their advantage. For example, a diver will jump high into the air to perform a somersault. If he is planning to do many spins, such as in a $2\frac{1}{2}$ back somersault, the diver will often go into a "tuck" position, with arms and legs close to the body to increase the speed of the spin. After the diver has completed the $2\frac{1}{2}$ rotations, he will extend his arms and legs to slow the spin and enter the water vertically.

the mass of the object times its speed times the radius of the circle the object is moving in. In this activity, once you have been pushed, you spin in the chair with a specific amount of angular momentum that won't change unless acted on by an outside force. Since the mass stays the same during the entire activity, the only things that can change are the speed and radius of the circle. When you bring the weights closer to your body, you decrease the radius in which you are rotating. Something has to compensate for this decrease, so your speed increases to maintain the same amount of angular momentum.

But if angular momentum is conserved, why do you slow down and stop? You could spin forever if there were no other forces acting on you, but there are. Friction in the chair and air resistance slow you down, and you eventually stop.

An ice-skater can begin a spin with her hands out, creating a large radius. As she brings her arms closer to her body, she shortens their radius of rotation, so she begins to spin faster. The closer her arms are to her body, the faster she spins. When she wants to slow the spin down, she simply extends her arms to reverse the process.

Project 3
TAKING OFF

Sometimes athletes on skis and snowboards seem to defy gravity. Competitors speed down a snowy hill, then throw themselves into the air. From there, they might glide for great distances or do acrobatic flips. To learn more about how science influences their jumps, try this activity.

Materials
12-by-24-inch (30-by-60-cm) piece of thin cardboard
several books
marble

Procedure
1. Make two piles of books next to each other near the edge of a table. Make one pile about 6 inches (15 cm) high and the other about 12 inches (30 cm) high.

2. Place one edge of the cardboard even with the edge of the smaller pile of books. Lay the cardboard down so that the rest of the cardboard makes a smooth ramp up the taller pile of books.

3. Hold the ramp in place with one hand and release the marble at the top of the cardboard ramp. What does the marble do?

4. Make two piles of books about 6 inches (15 cm) high and about 12 inches (30 cm) apart.

5. Position the cardboard between the books so that it extends equally up each pile of books and forms a half cylinder in the space between the books.

6. Hold a marble at the edge of the pile of books and drop it so that it falls on one end of the cardboard half cylinder. What does the marble do this time?

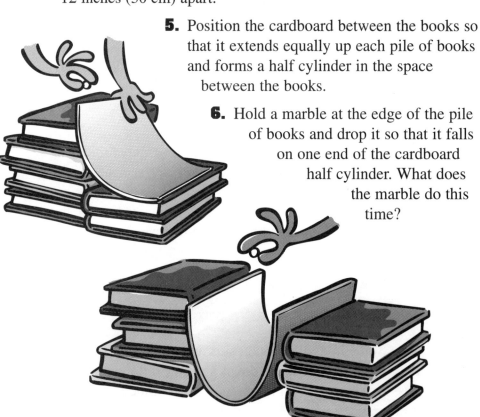

More Fun Stuff to Do

Try making other shapes with the cardboard or use larger pieces of cardboard as ramps for the marble. What paths do the marbles take?

Explanation

In the first part of the activity, the marble will roll down the ramp and will fly off the end, landing on the floor below. In the second part, the marble will roll up the half cylinder, stop, then roll back down.

This activity shows how the shape of a ramp affects objects that move down it. The first part of the activity simulates a ski jump hill and the second part simulates a snowboard half-pipe. When the marble is held to begin the activity, it has gravitational potential energy because of its position above Earth. When it is released, this potential energy is turned into kinetic energy, the energy of motion. Objects pulled by gravity accelerate (increase in speed), so the marbles roll fastest at the bottom of each hill.

SPORTS SCIENCE IN ACTION

Although ski jumpers travel a long distance in the air, with some jumpers traveling over 300 feet (91 m), they never get higher than a few yards off the surface of the snow. This is because as they travel forward and down, the hill is also curving away from them. Their downward speed continues to increase because of gravity and they eventually land far down the hill.

On the first ramp, the speed of the marble levels off when it begins traveling horizontally at the bottom of the ramp. When the marble falls off the edge of the cardboard, gravity again causes the marble to fall toward the ground with increasing speed. However, because the marble still has horizontal velocity, it will travel in a curved path, eventually hitting the ground.

PATH OF SKIER

CURVE OF MOUNTAIN

LANDING AREA

In ski jumping, a skier glides down a ramp with her body leaning slightly forward. The instant the skier reaches the end of the ramp, she jumps and becomes airborne. Once in the air, the ski jumper tries to maximize her aerodynamic shape by keeping her skis up and in a V position, her back flat, and her body parallel to the skis with her heels slightly lower than her hips. This decreases air resistance and causes a ski jumper to travel farther in the air. (When ski jumpers land in competition, they are required to position one leg in front of the other and bend forward as they touch the landing hill. This is called a "telemark" landing.)

In the second part of the activity, the marble also reaches its fastest speed at the bottom of the hill but then has to roll up the hill on the other side of the half cylinder. When it rolls uphill, its kinetic energy is converted back into potential energy. The marble slows, stops, then rolls back the other way, where the process is repeated. Some of the energy is converted to heat due to friction until the marble finally stops at the bottom of the half cylinder.

Snowboarding's half-pipe event takes place in a U-shaped, half-cylinder course similar to the half cylinder you made for your marble. Competitors ride back and forth from one edge of the pipe to the other while performing aerial tricks and jumps.

Project 4
GIVING THEM THE SLIP

You may have watched skiers and snowboarders doing something to their skis and boards before they start a race. Do you know what they are doing and why? Try this activity to find out.

Materials

2 wooden boards each 1 by 4 by 24 inches (2.5 by 10 by 60 cm)
paraffin wax (available at grocery stores)
ruler
ice cubes

Procedure

1. Rub one side of one of the boards with the paraffin wax until the entire side is well covered.

2. Place the board without wax flat on the table. Hold the ruler vertically near one end of the board.

3. Place an ice cube at the same end of the board as the ruler.

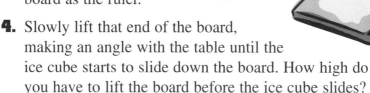

4. Slowly lift that end of the board, making an angle with the table until the ice cube starts to slide down the board. How high do you have to lift the board before the ice cube slides?

5. Now place the waxed board on the table with the waxed side up and hold the ruler vertically near it. Place an ice cube on that end of the board.

6. Repeat step 4 and slowly lift that end of the board. How high do you have to lift the board before the ice cube slides? Is it more or less than the unwaxed board?

More Fun Stuff to Do

Try painting one side of the board with enamel paint and then waxing it. Does this have any effect on the height the board must be raised before the ice cube slides? Can you think of anything else you could do to the board to make the ice cube slide more easily?

Explanation

The ice cube will slide down the waxed board when that board is held up at a lower height than the unwaxed board. Painting the board with enamel paint will also lower the height that the board must be raised to cause the ice cube to slide.

This activity shows the effect of friction on moving objects. Friction is a force that resists motion whenever one material rubs against the surface of another. The rougher the surface, the more force is needed to move it against another surface, so the friction is stronger. When you wax the surface of the board, you make it smoother and decrease friction, making it easier for the ice cube to slide down the board.

Skiers and snowboarders will wax the bottoms of their skis and boards to decrease the friction between them and the snow so they move faster down the hills. Surfers and water-skiers also wax their skis and boards for the same reason. For more about water sports, see chapter 5.

SPORTS SCIENCE IN ACTION

Decreasing friction as much as possible isn't good for all kinds of skiing. In cross-country skiing, the skier must be able to travel across flat ground. To do this the skier "runs" on the snow as well as glides, so she needs to be able to grip the snow and push off with one ski while shifting her body weight to glide on the other.

Cross-country skiers use wax on their skis, but it's different from that used by downhill skiers. Cross-country ski waxes are basically a blend of oil resins and paraffin wax. The exact kind of wax used depends on the temperature and the kind of snow the skier will be skiing on. Cross-country skiers put on a layer of wax that is just slightly softer than the snow crystals themselves. This way the edges of the crystals penetrate into the layer of wax during the time the racer is pushing off. After the skier pushes off, the bond between the wax and snow breaks and the ski glides forward on a very thin layer of water created by the heat of friction between the ski and snow.

STABLE BASE

You may have noticed that skiers, snowboarders, speed skaters, and many other athletes begin with a similar body position in which they spread their feet and bend their knees. Why do they use this position? Try this activity to find out.

Materials

3 cardboard rectangles—each 10 by 12 inches (25 by 30 cm)
ruler
pencil
scissors
adult helper

Procedure

1. On one of the cardboard rectangles, draw a diagonal line connecting opposite corners. Have the adult helper cut along the line to create a right triangle. A right triangle is a triangle that has one angle of 90 degrees.

2. On another of the cardboard rectangles, place the ruler along one of the 10-inch (25-cm) sides. Make a mark along the edge that is 5 inches (12.5 cm) from one corner. Connect that mark to the opposite corners of the rectangle. Have the adult helper cut along the lines to create an isosceles triangle. An isosceles triangle is a triangle in which two sides have the same length.

3. Stand the remaining cardboard rectangle on edge so that one shorter end is on the floor and one face of the rectangle is toward you.

4. Place your index finger in the middle of the top edge of the rectangle. Slowly rotate the rectangle by moving your finger to the left. How far does the cardboard have to rotate before it falls over to the left?

5. Repeat steps 3 and 4, starting this time with the cardboard right triangle standing on the shorter edge and the right angle (90 degrees) on the left side. How far does this cardboard figure have to rotate before it falls over?

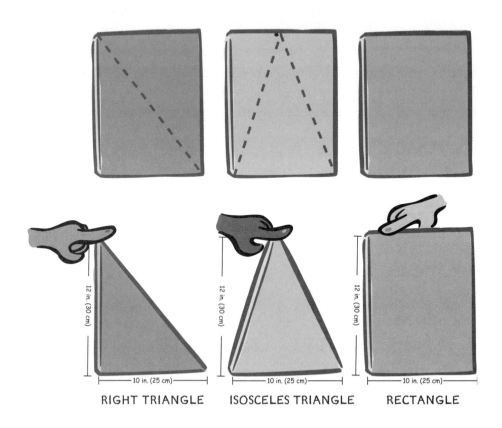

RIGHT TRIANGLE   ISOSCELES TRIANGLE   RECTANGLE

6. Repeat steps 3 and 4, using the cardboard isosceles triangle standing on the shorter edge. How far does this board have to rotate before it falls over?

More Fun Stuff to Do

Stand straight up with your feet together and have a helper push you gently from the side. Is it easy or hard to push you over? Next, spread your feet and bend your knees and have the helper push you gently from the side. Is it easier or harder to push you over?

Explanation

It should be easiest to push the cardboard right triangle over, and harder to push the rectangle over. It should be hardest to push the isosceles triangle over. In the More Fun Stuff to Do activity, it should also be harder to push you over when your feet are spread and your knees are bent.

One factor that makes any object, such as a building or a standing person, stay upright is the relationship of the object's center of gravity to its support base. The center of gravity of an object is the point in the object around which its weight is evenly distributed, where the force of gravity can be considered to act. If the center of gravity is above the area of support, the structure will remain upright. If the center of gravity extends outside of its support base, the structure is unstable and will have a tendency to fall over. As an object leans over, its center of gravity moves. When it moves far enough out so that it is no longer over the support base, the object will fall over. The support area for a structure does not have to be solid. For example, if your legs form a triangular area, then that area becomes the support base for your body.

SPORTS SCIENCE IN ACTION

Some winter sports go back thousands of years. But snowboarding started less than 40 years ago. In 1964, Sherman Poppen, of Muskegon, Michigan, built the first snowboard after watching his daughter try to slide down a hill while standing on her sled. Poppen's invention became popular enough for a local manufacturer to begin production of the "Snurfer" board. But it was 14-year-old Jake Burton Carpenter who, after using the Snurfer, decided it could use some modifications. By the time he was 23, in 1977, Carpenter founded Burton Snowboards, now the world's largest snowboard manufacturer.

Rolling Right Along

4

Wheel Sports

any sports, from NASCAR racing to skateboarding, involve riding on wheels. A wheel and axle is a form of simple machine. A **machine** is any device that helps people do work (or participate in sports) more easily. For example, you could run a mile or you could use a bicycle to ride that mile much faster and easier. Every machine performs at least one of the following functions. A bicycle does them all, as you'll see.

1. A machine may transfer forces from one place to another. The chain of a bicycle transfers the force from the pedals to the rear wheel.

2. A machine may change the direction of a force. The levers and cable system that are used to change gears will allow you to pull a gear lever back to move the chain up.

3. A machine may multiply speed or distance. The different-size chain sprockets on a bicycle change the speed you can ride. Your legs can pedal at one speed, but with a large gear on the pedal sprocket and a small gear on the chain sprockets, you turn the wheels at a much faster speed.

4. A machine may multiply force. If you put a small gear on the pedal sprocket and the large gear on the rear wheel, then a smaller force on the pedals creates a larger force on the rear wheel and you can pedal up a steep hill.

To learn more about how things with wheels help you do sports, try the activities in this chapter.

Project 1
TURNING AROUND

Have you ever wondered why the pedal gears and the rear wheel gears on a bicycle are different sizes? Try the next activity to learn why.

Materials

wooden board
hammer
finishing nails

thread spools, various sizes
rubber bands
adult helper

Procedure

1. Have your adult helper hammer two nails partway into the piece of wood. Place equal-size thread spools on each nail, as shown below. Stretch a rubber band around the spool.

2. Turn one spool. What direction does the other spool turn?

3. Make a mark on the ends of each spool. Turn one spool exactly one full turn. How much does the other spool turn?

4. Replace one of the spools with a larger spool and repeat the steps above, this time turning the larger spool. How many times does the smaller spool turn with one full turn of the larger spool? How is this arrangement different from when you did it with two spools that were the same size?

More Fun Stuff to Do

Try using different-size spools for the activity. What combination of spools turns the second spool the farthest when you turn the first spool one full turn?

Explanation

When the spools are the same size, one turn of the first spool will give you one turn of the second spool. When the spools are a different size and you turn the larger spool one full turn, the smaller speed will turn more than one full turn. In the More Fun Stuff to Do activity, if the first spool is very large and the second is very small, the second spool will turn the most for each turn of the larger spool.

Thread spools that are linked together with rubber bands have a lot in common with the gears and chain mechanism on a bicycle. The movement of the first spool is transferred by the rubber band to the other spool, just as the movement of the pedals of your bicycle is transferred by the chain to the rear wheel, causing it to turn.

A **gear** is a toothed wheel. Gears are usually fastened to axles or shafts and are used to transfer circular, or rotational, motion from one shaft to another. In doing this, gears change the direction of the applied force (you push down on your pedals and the wheels move your bicycle forward). They may also change the magnitude of the force.

When two same-size spools (or gears that are the same size with the same number of teeth) are connected, the turning of one will cause the other one to also turn in the same direction and at the same speed.

SPORTS SCIENCE IN ACTION

One of the first bicycles was known as the high wheeler or penny-farthing of the late 1800s. Early bicycles had one large wheel on the front of the cycle and a smaller wheel at the back. They didn't use a gear and chain system. Instead the rider would turn pedals attached to the front wheel, similar to a tricycle. With a very large front wheel, a single turn of the smaller pedal circle caused the large front wheel to make one full turn. Since the front wheel was so much bigger than the pedal circle, this meant that for a single pedal circle, the cycle might move up to 140 inches (3.5 m), a tremendous distance. Cyclers could pedal with an average speed of 20 mph (32 km/h) on flat ground. However, these bicycles were difficult to pedal uphill, and the riders where so high off the ground it was very dangerous if the cycler fell! When gear and chain bicycles were first used in 1887 in the Victor Bicycle, they quickly replaced the high wheeler.

However, if the spools or gears are different sizes (or the gears have a different number of teeth), the results are different and the amount they turn is different. If a larger spool (or gear) turns a smaller spool (or gear), the smaller gear will turn more turns than the larger gear. If the spools (or gears) were spinning, the smaller spool (or gear) would turn faster and the larger spool (or gear) would turn slower. In this way, spools, such as the ones you used in this activity or the gears on your bicycle, can be used to change the speed of motion.

Project 2
GEARING UP

If you have a bicycle with several gears, you know that some gears can make it easier to pedal uphill while others will let you travel faster on level ground. How do these gears work? Try this activity to find out.

Materials

bicycle
masking tape

Procedure

1. Put the bicycle in a low gear, using the largest sprocket on the rear wheel gears and the smallest sprocket on the pedal gears.

2. Turn your bicycle upside down so that it rests on its handlebars and its seat. Place a piece of masking tape on the rear tire as a marker.

3. Count the number of gear teeth on the front sprocket and on the back sprocket that you are using. Write the values down.

4. Divide the number of teeth on the front sprocket by the number of teeth on the rear sprocket. Record the value.

5. Turn the pedal crank one full turn. Watch the tape on the rear tire. How many times does the rear wheel turn?

6. Next put the bicycle in a high gear, using the smallest sprocket on the rear wheel.

7. Count the number of gear teeth on the back sprocket that you are using this time and write this value down.

8. Divide the number of teeth on the front sprocket by the number of teeth on the rear sprocket. Record the value.

9. Again turn the pedal crank one full turn. Watch the tape on the rear tire. How many times does the rear wheel turn?

More Fun Stuff to Do

Put on your bicycle helmet and go out for a ride. Ride your bicycle uphill. Which gear makes it easiest to go up the hill? Ride your bicycle as fast as you can on level ground. Which gear helps you go the fastest?

Explanation

When you use the largest sprocket on the rear wheel, the ratio of the number of teeth on the front gear divided by the number of teeth on the rear gear will be a small number, and one turn of the pedal will turn the rear wheel only a few times. However, when you use the smallest sprocket on the rear wheel, the ratio of the number of teeth on the front gear divided by the number of teeth on the rear gear will be a larger number, and one turn of the pedal will turn the rear wheel more times.

The way that the gears and chain work on a bicycle depends entirely on the sizes of the two sprockets and, in this case, on the number of teeth each has. As you learned in the previous activity, in any pair of gears, the larger gear will rotate more slowly than the smaller gear, but it will rotate with greater force. The bigger the difference in size between the two gears, the bigger the difference in speed and force.

The gears of a bicycle allow you to make trades between the force you need to push the pedals and distance you can go with each push. The ratio of front sprocket teeth to back sprocket teeth in low gears means that the rear tire will turn fewer times for one pedal turn when compared to higher gears. But you need less force to make the pedal turn. This is helpful on hills, where you may not be able to ride in higher gears because you are using more force to fight against gravity. In higher gears the rear tire will turn more times for one pedal turn when compared to lower gears. So higher gears allow you to go greater distances on level ground with fewer pedal turns.

SPORTS SCIENCE IN ACTION

Technology continues to improve the design of the bicycle. In part, this is due to the desire to make bicycles go faster in sports events, such as pursuit cycling, in which individual riders or riding teams start on opposite sides of a track and try to catch up to one another. The newest pursuit bicycle cost $5 million to develop. Its frame is made of lightweight carbon fibers, and its tires are inflated to 250 pounds per square inch, $2\frac{1}{2}$ times greater than the pressure in normal bicycle tires. This "superbike" had its aerodynamic efficiency studied in a wind tunnel at a cost of $40,000 per hour!

Project 3
CAUGHT IN THE DRAFT

The most famous bicycle race in the world is the Tour de France, in which racers cover over 2,500 miles (4,000 km) of road over mountains and through the French countryside in three weeks. The race is an all-out test of riders' speed, strategy, and heart.

Have you ever watched this or another bicycle race and wondered why the riders usually ride in a pack? Try this activity to find out.

Materials

candle   pie plate

matches   adult helper

Procedure

1. Have your adult helper light the candle with the matches.

2. Hold the candle in front of you, in your right hand, and slowly turn in a circle to the left so that the candle moves from right to left. What direction does the candle flame move?

3. Return to your starting position. Again hold the lighted candle in your right hand. This time hold the pie plate in your left hand, about 18 inches (45 cm) to the left of the candle.

4. Slowly turn in a circle to the left so that the pie plate stays 18 inches (45 cm) to the left the candle. What direction does the candle flame move this time?

5. Return to your starting position. Again hold the lighted candle in your right hand and the pie plate in your left hand, but this time hold the pie plate about 4 inches (10 cm) to the left of the candle.

6. Slowly turn in a circle to the left so that the pie plate stays 4 inches (10 cm) to the left of the candle. What direction does the candle flame move this time?

Explanation

As you turn to the left with the candle alone, the candle flame will move to the right. When you hold the pie plate 18 inches (45 cm) from the candle, the flame will still move to the right. But when the candle is 4 inches (10 cm) from the pie plate and they are moved to the left together, the candle flame will also move left.

This activity shows the importance of aerodynamics in bicycle racing. **Aerodynamics** is the study of the forces exerted by air and other gases in motion. When the candle moved through the air, the air pushed on the candle flame and the flame moved in a direction opposite to the motion. When an object, such as the pie plate, moves through the air, the air moves around it. As the air moves behind it, the air begins to spin and produces a turbulent wake that rejoins itself later on. When the pie plate was 18 inches (45 cm) away from the candle, the air disturbed by the object had rejoined so the flame still moved in the direction opposite the way the candle was moving. But when the candle was 4 inches from the pie plate, it was caught in the wake created by the air moving around the pie plate. The air in the wake spins and moves in the same direction as the pie plate, and the candle flame moves in the same direction as the candle.

Drafting in bicycle racing occurs when one cyclist rides right behind another in the front rider's wake. It is an important technique in road racing. The front cyclist, as he moves through the air, produces **vortices** (an area of spinning air) and a wake where the air moves in the same direction as the cyclist. Because the air in the vortices spins faster than the rest of the air, it creates an area of low pressure due to Bernoulli's principle. (For more information on Bernoulli's principle see chapter 2, Curveball.) The rear cyclist can use the vortices and wake to his advantage if he rides right behind the front cycler. With a low pressure, created by the vortices, in front of the rear cyclist and higher pressure behind, the pressure difference will push the cyclist forward. Also, the air in the wake will move in the same direction as the cycling and push him along as well.

In road racing, such as the Tour de France, bicyclists group together in a pack known as the *peleton* or a pace line called an "echelon." Cyclists who are part of these groups can save up to 40 percent of their energy by using the vortices and wakes of the front riders to push them along. To be most effective, a cyclist needs to be as close as possible to the bicycle in front of him, often riding within a few inches.

Project 4
KEEP ON ROLLING ALONG

When you are in a bicycle race, you want to get moving as fast as possible. As you saw in previous activities, having a bicycle with gears will help. Try this activity to see how wheel design can help a bicycle roll faster.

Materials

2 same-size smooth, cylindrical plastic soda bottles (clean and dry) with screw-on caps
sidewalk with a slight incline
water

Procedure

1. Place both plastic bottles on their sides, near the top of the inclined sidewalk. Release each and let them roll down the incline. Do they roll in a straight line? If not, try to find two bottles that can roll in a straight line.

2. Fill one bottle completely with water. Screw the cap on tightly.

3. Place the bottles next to each other, on their sides, at the top of the incline.

4. Release both bottles at the same time. Which bottle rolls the fastest down the hill?

More Fun Stuff to Do

Try rolling similar cans that have different foods inside them. For example, try cans of soup and peaches. What influence do the contents of the cans have on the speed the cans have rolling down the hill? Which cans roll the fastest?

Explanation

When the two bottles roll down the hill, the bottle that is filled with water will roll faster than the bottle that is empty. In the More Fun Stuff to Do activity, the can that has more solid contents, such as beans or chili, will often roll faster than a similar can filled with a food that is more liquid and can move freely around in the can.

This activity is another example of the law of angular momentum. Remember that this law says that an object rotating on its axis will keep moving at that same speed around the axis unless acted on by an outside force. Angular momentum is not necessarily a fixed quantity for any object but depends on the mass of the object, the speed it rotates, and the distance the mass is from the axis of rotation. To complicate matters, the angular momentum depends on how the mass is distributed in an object as well. If the mass in a circular object is located around the outside rim it has more rotational inertia than a similar object that is solid and has its mass spread evenly throughout. The bottle filled with water has its mass spread evenly throughout the bottle and thus has less angular momentum than the empty bottle. Therefore, its speed increases more easily.

Designers of racing bicycles experiment with different wheel designs to see what is the best way to attach the rim to the axle. With a regular spoke design, the mass of the wheel is concentrated around the edge of the rim. This kind of wheel has a higher rotational inertia than a wheel that has its mass spread more evenly. New wheels have been designed in which a solid material connects the rim to the axle. These wheels have lower rotational inertia and also decrease the effects of air resistance on the spokes, making the wheels roll easier and faster.

Project 5
PUMPING

On flat ground, the easiest way to get a skateboard moving faster is to push off with one foot. But how do you get a skateboard to move faster when you are in a half-pipe? The answer lies in a trick you may have done while swinging on playground swings—pumping. To learn more about pumping, try this activity.

Materials

18-inch (45-cm) piece of string
small plastic figure

Procedure

1. Tie the plastic figure to one end of the piece of string. The string and figure will be used as a pendulum.

2. Hold the free end of the string in your left hand so that the pendulum hangs in front of you.

3. Use your right hand to pull the plastic figure several inches to the right, keeping the string taut.

4. Keeping your left hand still, let the plastic figure go. Watch the figure as it swings. What happens to the amount of swing the plastic figure goes through?

5. Begin the process again, but this time, when the plastic figure reaches the bottom of its swing, lift the string up an inch (2.5 cm) or so. As the pendulum continues its arc and begins to rise, return the pendulum and string to their normal height.

6. Continue this rise and fall of the pendulum for each swing. What happens to the amount of swing the plastic figure goes through this time?

Explanation

When you first let go, the plastic figure will swing in an arc. The arc gets smaller and smaller with each swing. But when you lift the figure when the figure reaches the bottom of its arc, the figure will swing through a larger and larger arc.

Pumping is important in both getting a swing to swing higher and in getting a skateboarder in a half-pipe to travel higher and faster up the inclines. With **pumping,** you are raising an object's center of mass. This is more obvious with the pendulum but is also true for pumping a swing or a skateboard. When you lift the swinging plastic

SPORTS SCIENCE IN ACTION

There are many skateboard tricks for which riders need to generate great speed in a half-pipe. When skateboarders are moving fast enough, they are able to lift off beyond the top edge of the half-pipe and into the air, where they can perform acrobatic tricks and spins before gravity pulls them back to Earth.

Some tricks, such as a 900, are named after the actions a skater takes (a 900-degree spin while in the air). Others are named by the first person who performs it. When skateboarder Tony Hawk was in Sweden working at a skateboard camp, a camper peeked in Tony's notebook where he wrote about new moves he was working on. When the camper later asked Tony about his "Stalefish" move, Tony laughed. He hadn't been writing about a new move but the food served for lunch that day! However, Tony liked the name and used it for his next move.

figure at the bottom of its arc, you raise its center of mass and give it more gravitational potential energy. As the figure moves up the arc and you return the string to its normal height, that extra potential energy is converted into kinetic energy, the energy of motion. Because the figure gained kinetic energy each time you pulled the string up, the plastic figure swung higher and higher.

To pump in a half-pipe, a skateboarder first goes into a crouch position while traveling in the bottom of the U-shaped pipe. As she begins to travel up the sides of the pipe, she straightens her legs and rises up. By raising her center of mass at the beginning of the ramp's arc, the skater increases her gravitational potential energy. The potential energy is then converted to kinetic energy, causing the skateboarder to move faster and travel farther up the pipe.

Project 6
JUMP INTO HISTORY

Have you ever watched a skateboarder who is really good and wondered how he does his fancy moves? He may do an ollie, a no-hands aerial, in which he pops the board up from the tail and the board seems to stick to his feet in the air. How does he do it? Try this activity to see.

Materials

wooden board—$\frac{3}{4}$ by 10 by 24 inches (2 by 25 by 60 cm)
wooden broom handle—at least 12 inches (30 cm) long

Procedure

1. Place the broom handle on the floor.

2. Place the board on the handle so that its width runs the same direction as the handle.

3. Slide the board along the handle until one end is about 6 inches (15 cm) from the handle.

4. Stand on the board with your right foot near the short end of the board and the left about 18 inches (45 cm) away.

5. Shift your body slightly so that most of your weight is on your left foot. What happens to the right end of the board?

6. Shift your body again so that most of your weight is now on your right foot. What happens to the left side of the board?

7. Shift your weight rapidly from your left foot to your right foot. What happens to the left side of the board?

More Fun Stuff to Do

After putting on a helmet, knee pads, wrist guards, and other protective gear, try this activity on your skateboard. Shift your weight to your left foot and then quickly to your right foot. Can you make the skateboard's rear wheels leave the ground?

Explanation

When your shift your weight to your left foot, the right side of the board will move up. When you shift your weight to your right foot, the right side of the board will move down and the left side of the board will move up. If you shift your weight from your left foot to your right foot, the left end of the board (or your skateboard in the More Fun Stuff to Do) will bounce up higher than normal.

The board and handle form a lever, as do the rear wheels and board of a skateboard. A lever is a simple machine made up of a rigid board or bar that is supported at a fixed point called a fulcrum. Levers make it easier to lift heavy loads because they magnify the force exerted. They can turn a small force into a big one.

To lift a heavy load with a lever, you would set the load at a place near one end of the lever and position the fulcrum near it. The exact force needed to lift the load will depend on the length of the lever and the location of the fulcrum. In the case of this activity, when your right foot is near the fulcrum, you can lift it with only part of your weight on your left foot. But when you shift your weight to your right foot, you do two things. You increase the force on the right side of the board and you decrease the load on the other side. This causes the left side of the board to move upward very quickly.

Invented in the late 1970s by Alan "Ollie" Gelfand, the ollie has become a skateboarding fundamental, the basis for many other more complicated tricks. The ollie is a jumping technique that allows skaters to jump obstacles while their feet seem to be stuck to the board. But to jump up, the skater pushes down on the board, just like you did in this activity. From a crouched position, the skater straightens his legs and raises his arms. His rear, right foot pushes the tail of the board down, and the nose of the board rises quickly. As the tail strikes the ground, the force bounces the tail of the board up as well and the entire skateboard is off the ground. With the skateboard completely in the air, the skater pushes his front foot down and lifts his back foot, as the rear wheels rise up under him, thus leveling the board in the air. If this motion is perfectly timed, it seems like the board is stuck to his feet during the jump. With both the board and skater in the air, gravity pulls them both down at the same rate, and the skater lands on his skateboard back on the ground.

5 Splish, Splash

Water Sports

ater, or H$_2$O, is made of two parts of hydrogen and one part of oxygen. Water covers 70 percent of the surface of the Earth and is needed by all living things. We find water in a solid form (ice and snow), a liquid form (water), and even a gas (steam). In chapter 3 you learned how ice and snow are used in sports like skiing and snowboarding. In this chapter you'll learn how water is used in sports such as surfing and boating.

Water has interesting properties that affect how water sports work, including surface tension, buoyancy, pressure, and waves. Why do boats float? What's the best shape for a boat's hull? How do you sail into the wind? How does a surfboard ride on a wave? To find out, try the activities in this chapter.

Project 1
WATER SKIN

Watch a surfer or a water-skier gliding on the surface of the water. How do they stay up there? Try this activity to learn one important property of water that makes both of these sports possible.

Materials

drinking glass
tap water
2 paper clips

Procedure

1. Fill the glass with water.

2. Unfold one of the paper clips to create a hook with a flat surface as shown.

3. Place the other paper clip on the flat surface of the unfolded paper clip hook. Hold the second paper clip horizontally above the water, as close as possible to the surface of the water but without touching it.

4. Slowly lower the paper clip into the water. What happens?

Note: If the paper clip doesn't float on the surface of the water, try rubbing it against a candle before lowering it into the water.

More Fun Stuff to Do

Try floating other metal objects on the surface of the water. Can you float a sewing needle or a small metal washer on the surface of the water?

Explanation

The paper clip will float on the surface of the water.

The paper clip floats on the surface of the water because of a special property of water called **surface tension.** Molecules of some substances, such as water, are attracted to one another. They are called polar molecules because each molecule has a positive end and a negative end. The positive part of one molecule is attracted to the negative part of another. Each water molecule is attracted in all directions to the water molecules next to it. However, water molecules on the surface of the water have no molecules above them, so they are only attracted to those next to and underneath them. This attraction creates a tension like a thin skin on the surface of the water. The surface tension of water is strong enough to support the paper clip.

Both water-skiers and surfers use surface tension to help keep them on top of the water. After the water ski or the surfboard reaches a fast enough speed to get the ski or board out of the water and onto the surface, the surface tension of the water helps to keep the ski and board there.

RIDING THE WAVES

The sport of surfing originated in Hawaii. Originally, surfing had tremendous social significance. Great chiefs from various tribes participated in national surfing contests. Hawaii is still a great place to surf because of all the large waves that reach the island's shores. Try this activity to learn more about waves and how surfboards ride on them.

Materials

masking tape   smooth floor
Slinky   helper

Procedure

1. Wrap a piece of masking tape around one spot on the Slinky to act as a marker.

2. You and your helper should hold opposite ends of the Slinky and stretch it out on a smooth floor. You should be at least 15 feet (5 m) apart.

3. With your helper holding her end of the Slinky still, move your end of the Slinky back and forth quickly. What happens? What does the piece of tape do?

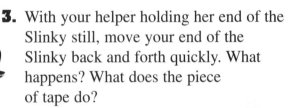

More Fun Stuff to Do

Create waves with your Slinky again as you did in step I but this time move your end of the slinky back and forth more quickly. What happens this time?

Explanation

Moving your hand back and forth makes a wave in the Slinky that moves away from you. However, the masking tape will only move up and down. If you move your hand back and forth faster, as in the More Fun Stuff to Do activity, the wave will move faster as well, but the tape will still only move up and down.

A wave is a way to transfer energy from one place to another. The highest point of a wave is called a **crest** while the lowest point is called a **trough.** The distance between wave crests is the **wavelength** of the wave, and the distance from the middle of the wave to its crest is the wave's **amplitude.** In this activity, you created a **transverse wave,** a wave that moves perpendicular to its source. You moved your hand up and down to create a wave that moved away from you. An ocean wave is also a transverse wave.

The main wave-building force on the ocean is wind. The force of the wind against the ocean's surface causes areas of the ocean to move upward, creating swells. (Later, these swells will form the crest of a wave.) The swells begin to move out like ripples around a pebble dropped in a pond. Like the wave in the slinky, the swell (and its energy) moves out, but the water molecules in one spot only move up and down. As the swells enter shallow coastal waters, ridable waves begin to form. When the water depth is about one-half the wavelength, the incoming swell begins to get resistance from the ocean floor. Because of this resistance, the swell slows down and the distance between crests decreases. As this happens, the back of the wave begins to catch the front of the wave, making the wave begin to grow taller. The front of the wave becomes steeper, and the crest of the wave begins to fall forward in what is called a **break.**

Surfing is a lot like riding a skateboard down a hill, with the added advantage that the hill is moving along with you. When a surfer wants to ride a wave, she first paddles her surfboard to the place in

Long before Captain Cook sailed into Kealakekua Bay in 1778, Hawaiians had mastered the art of standing erect on a surfboard while speeding toward shore. These early surfboards were carved from solid wood, were up to 15 feet (4.5 m) long, and weighed as much as 150 pounds (68 kg). These boards were difficult to paddle, and it was thought by many that only Hawaiians could master the sport of surfing. For a long time few people tried. But by the beginning of the 20th century, boards had begun to shrink in size and decrease in weight, and surfing started to become popular with school-age students. In 1907, George Freeth, a young Irish-Hawaiian, moved to Southern California, where he popularized surfing on the mainland. After World War II, Southern California became the center for surfboard experimentation. Surfboard designers added a skeg, or tail fin, to their boards (to keep the board from side slipping on steep waves) and an ankle leash (to keep from having to swim after your surfboard when you fell off). New boards were made of lightweight balsa wood or Styrofoam covered with a hard coating of fiberglass mixed with resin (to make the board both light and strong). This combination produced faster, lighter, and more maneuverable surfboards that more people could ride.

the water where the waves will break. As a swell arrives, the surfer and surfboard rise upward with the swell, which increases their gravitational potential energy. The surfer then paddles in the same direction the wave is breaking. As the wave front gets steeper, the surfboard begins to slide down the face of the wave. As the surfer and surfboard move down the face of the wave, their gravitational potential energy is converted into kinetic energy, the energy of motion, and the surfboard moves faster and faster. When the board is moving fast enough, the surfer stands up on the board and rides the wave either straight down or diagonally across the face of the wave, moving at the same speed as the wave and keeping just ahead of the breaking foam.

ROW, ROW, ROW YOUR BOAT

Besides surface tension, water also has buoyancy, which keeps objects, such as boats and surfboards, from sinking. Buoyancy is the upward force that water creates on an object that counters the force of gravity pulling the object down. Buoyancy explains why a boat made of steel will float. Try this activity to find out how.

Materials

tub of water
2 identical Styrofoam cups
marbles

Procedure

1. Fill the tub half full of water.

2. Place one Styrofoam cup upright on the surface of the water.

3. Begin adding marbles to the cup. Add the marbles evenly to the cup so that the top of the cup remains level with the surface of the water. Keep adding marbles until the top of the cup is just even with the surface of the water.

4. Remove the cup with the marbles from the water.

5. Fill the second cup to the top with water.

6. Place one cup in each hand and compare the weight of each. Which weighs more, the cup with water or the cup with marbles?

More Fun Stuff to Do

Draw a line halfway up one Styrofoam cup and add marbles until the water level reaches that mark. Fill the second cup with water to a similar point and again compare the weights of the two cups. What do you notice?

Explanation

The cup filled with the marbles and the cup filled with water will have the same weight.

When an object, such as a boat, a surfboard, or even a cup filled with marbles, is placed in water, it displaces, or moves, some of the water. An object that is placed in water is held up by a force equal to the weight of the water that object displaces. This relationship is called **Archimedes' principle** and is the fundamental reason why things float. The upward buoyancy of the water on a boat is exactly equal to the force of gravity that pulls down on the boat so the boat floats.

Archimedes' principle is very important in the construction of a boat. The boat must always be built so that its weight is less than the weight of the volume of water it will displace.

SHAPES AND SPEED

The shape of an object has a great effect on how it moves through water. Boat designers try to find the best shape for their boat so that it moves smoothly through the water. Try this activity to see how the shape of a boat affects how it moves through water.

Materials

ruler
pencil
file folder or other stiff paper
scissors
cookie sheet (with sides)

water
toothpick
liquid dish soap
3 helpers

Procedure

1. Use the ruler and pencil to draw three identical 1-inch (2.5-cm) squares on the file folder.

2. Do nothing to the first square. At one end of the second square, draw a semicircle (half a circle) that has a radius of .5 inches

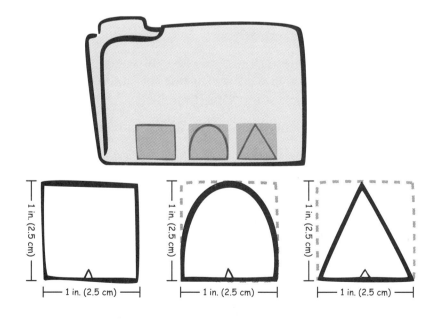

(1.25 cm). On the third square draw a triangle with both a height and base of 1 inch (2.5 cm).

3. Cut each shape out of the folder.

4. Cut a small notch out of the bottom end of each shape.

5. Fill the cookie sheet with a thin layer of water

6. Place the paper boats flat on the surface of the water at one edge of the cookie sheet.

7. Moisten the tips of three toothpicks with liquid dish soap. Give one to each of your helpers.

8. Have each person touch the water inside the notch of each boat with the wet toothpick at the same time.

9. Observe the movement of the boats. Which moves the fastest through the water?

More Fun Stuff to Do

Experiment with other shapes for the paper boats. Can you design a shape that moves faster than the original three?

Explanation

The soap causes the paper boats to move across the surface of the water because it breaks the surface tension of the water behind each boat. The surface tension that remains in front of the boat pulls the boat across the water. The boat with the pointed front should move fastest and the one with the square front should move the slowest.

The shape of an object affects the way it moves through both air and water. The more streamlined the shape, the faster the object can go. The study of shapes and how they affect the way an object moves through air or water is a field of science called aerodynamics. Water creates resistance, which works against things that move through them. Certain shapes will decrease this resistance. The bows of boats are shaped like pointed curves to allow them to decrease water resistance and more easily move through water.

SPORTS SCIENCE IN ACTION

In 1983, the longest winning streak in modern sports history ended when *Australia II* defeated the American boat *Liberty* in the America's Cup race, sailing's most prestigious contest. It was technology that helped *Australia II* win the race. The sailboat designers had added a radical and controversial "winged keel" to the bottom of the boat. Up to that time sailboats had a board that protruded straight down beneath the hull called a **keel.** The keel is used to help keep the boat traveling in a straight line and to keep the boat from tipping over when wind blows from the side. The winged keel added lateral fins, which acted like underwater airplane wings, to increase the *Australia II's* stability and speed.

Since then, new materials and technology have led to more new designs in America's Cup sailboats. In 1988, the American team's *Stars & Stripes* defended the cup using a 60-foot (18.2-m) ultralight **catamaran** (two-hulled boat) rather than a boat with a single hull. It was the first multihulled boat ever raced in the America's Cup. Also, rather than use a conventional sail made of a triangular pieces of cloth, the catamaran had a mast that looked like the wing of an airplane and was extremely efficient aerodynamically.

Project 5
SAILING INTO THE WIND

Have you ever watched a sailboat as it moves across the water? It is easy to understand how the boat moves when the wind is blowing from behind the boat. But how does the boat sail back into the wind? Try this activity to find out.

Materials

empty soda can
24 (2 dozen) plastic drinking straws

Procedure

1. Place the straws on the table. Set one straw aside. Spread the remaining 23 straws on the table parallel to one another and about ¼ to ½ inch (.625 to 1.25 cm) apart.

2. Stand the can on the straws but near the right edge of the straws.

3. Pick up the straw you set aside and point it at the left side of the can. Take a deep breath and blow a constant stream of air through the straw. What does the can do?

4. Keep blowing, moving your head and the straw so that it stays to the left of the can as the can moves.

Explanation

When you blow on the left side of the can, the can moves in that direction.

This activity demonstrates Bernoulli's principle, as explained in Curveball in chapter 2. Your blowing creates an area of low pressure on the left side of the can. The higher pressure pushing on the right side of the can causes the can to move to the left. The faster you blow, the lower the pressure, and the more the can will move.

The same force that moves the can also allow a sailboat to sail in the direction of the wind. When a sailboat sails into the wind it is called **tacking.** Although a boat cannot sail directly into the wind, it can sail in the general direction of the wind. Wind blowing from the front right of a sailboat will hit the mast and separate, flowing

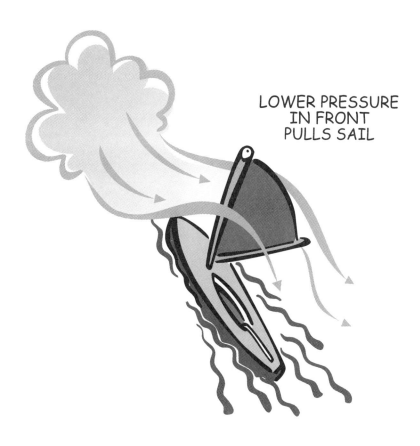

LOWER PRESSURE
IN FRONT
PULLS SAIL

around the mast and onto the mainsail. Some of the wind will move behind the sail, while the rest will move in front of the sail. If the sail is properly trimmed, or pulled into the correct position, the sail creates a curved surface. This curved surface causes the air flowing in front of the sail to travel faster, which creates a lower pressure. The result is a difference in air pressure between the front side and the back side of the sail. As a result, the sail (and the boat it is attached to) is pulled forward in the general direction of the wind.

Project 6
DOWN UNDER

Scuba diving is a sport that allows you to experience a whole new world, the world under the sea. **Scuba** is an acronym for Self-Contained Underwater Breathing Apparatus. The first scuba gear, or Aqua-Lung, was invented by the Frenchmen Jacques Yves Cousteau and Emil Gagnan in 1943. Since then, lighter, more afford-able scuba gear has made recreational diving possible for thousands of nonprofessional divers. The scuba diver wears tanks that carry a supply of pressurized breathing gas—either air or a mixture of oxy-gen and other gases. To learn more about underwater diving, try this next activity.

Materials
eyedropper
glass
water
$\frac{1}{2}$-gallon (2-liter) plastic soda bottle with screw-on lid (empty and washed)

Procedure
1. Put an eyedropper into a glass of water to make sure that it floats. Squeeze the bulb end and draw a small amount of water. If the dropper still floats, add more water. Keep adding or subtracting water until you get the dropper to just barely float upright in the water.

2. Fill the ¹/₂-gallon (2-liter) soda bottle to the very top with water. Make sure there are no air bubbles trapped inside the bottle.

3. Transfer the dropper into the bottle and push the dropper below the water's surface. Screw the lid tightly on the bottle.

4. Gently squeeze the bottle. What happens? Release the pressure on the bottle. What happens?

Explanation

When you squeeze the bottle, the eye-dropper will move toward the bottom of the bottle. When you release your pressure, the dropper will rise back to the surface.

This activity is an example of what happens with changing water pressure. When you squeeze the bottle, the water pressure inside the bottle increases, including the water pressure inside the eyedropper. As the water pressure inside the eyedropper increases, it pushes against the air inside the dropper. You can actually see the amount of water inside the dropper increase. As the water pressure inside the dropper rises, it squeezes the air in it into a smaller space, and more water moves into the dropper. This makes the dropper heavier than the water around it, so it sinks. When you release your squeeze, the water pressure in the bottle decreases, the air expands inside the dropper and returns to its normal level. The dropper becomes lighter than the surrounding water and starts to rise.

Imagine your eyedropper is a scuba diver. As a scuba diver moves down deeper in the water, she will encounter higher water pressure, similar to what you produced in this activity. Although some specially trained scuba divers can descend below 328 feet (100 m) for various kinds of work, recreational divers should never go below a depth of 130 feet (40 m) because of increased risk of nitrogen narcosis, a type of intoxication akin to drunkenness, or oxygen toxicity, which can cause blackouts or convulsions.

Another problem resulting from the increase in pressure under water is decompression sickness, more commonly called "the bends." This is a potentially lethal condition caused by swimming to the surface too rapidly. If a diver comes to the surface too quickly, there is less and less pressure on her body, so the air in her body expands rapidly.

This is similar to what happened when you released the pressure on the bottle. When the body goes from being under high water pressure to lower pressure quickly, nitrogen bubbles form in body fluids in a manner analogous to the fizzing that occurs when a bottle of carbonated beverage is uncapped. Fluids in the vicinity of large joints are especially susceptible to this bubbling, which causes severe, sometimes incapacitating, pain in those areas. Other symptoms include nausea and abdominal pain; in severe cases, coma and death result. To prevent the bends, divers time the rate they move to the surface according to a decompression schedule based both on the depth of the dive, the duration of the dive, and what the diver has been breathing.

SPORTS SCIENCE IN ACTION

The air we breathe on the surface of the Earth is about 80 percent nitrogen and 20 percent oxygen and is not safe to breathe at depths below 250 feet (76 m). This is because at that depth, the nitrogen can cause nitrogen narcosis. Pure oxygen is not safe either and can cause convulsions at depths below 66 feet (20 m). To prevent nitrogen narcosis and oxygen toxicity, deep-sea divers use carefully designed mixtures of oxygen and other gases such as helium, argon, neon, or hydrogen.

Project 7
SWIM LIKE A SHARK

In the past, on the days of major swimming events, some swimmers would shave all the hair off their bodies in order to decrease friction so that they could swim faster. In the 2000 Olympics, science went one step further and came up with a fabric that has even less friction than smooth human skin. To learn more about friction and water, try this activity.

Materials

several books
10-by-24-inch (25-by-60-cm) piece of wood
paraffin wax
two 4-by-12-inch (10-by-30-cm) pieces of cloth
eyedropper
water

Procedure

1. Stack the books in a pile on a table. Place one of the shorter ends of the piece of wood on the books to create a ramp.

2. Rub paraffin wax on one of the pieces of cloth to completely cover it.

3. Place the two pieces of cloth side by side on the wood.

4. Use an eyedropper to drop several drops of water on top of the untreated pieces of cloth. Observe the drops of water. What happens?

5. Place several drops of water on the top of the cloth that has been rubbed with wax. What happens to the drops of water this time?

More Fun Stuff to Do

Try repeating this activity but this time use different kinds of cloth, such as nylon and cotton. What kind of cloth causes the drop of water to roll down the hill the fastest?

Explanation

The drop of water on the piece of cloth rubbed with wax will move down the cloth faster than the drops placed on the untreated cloth.

This is another example of friction, similar to the Giving Them the Slip activity in chapter 3. This activity shows the effect of friction on moving objects. Remember that friction is a force that resists motion whenever one material rubs against the surface of another. This is true when a solid comes in contact with a liquid, such as when a swimmer moves through the water. The rougher the surface, the more force is needed to move it against another surface, so the friction is stronger. When you wax the surface of the cloth, you make it smoother and decrease friction, making it easier for the drops to slide down the cloth as it rests on the board. Also, wax is water resistant so water tends to move along the surface rather than soak into the cloth.

There are two ways that a swimmer can improve his time in a race. The first is to increase his propulsion and the second is to decrease his drag, or water resistance (a kind of friction). One kind of drag is called skin drag. When water moves across the surface of the body, it begins to move away from the skin, often because it hits hairs and small imperfections on the human body. This causes drag, and the swimmer slows slightly. In an event such as swimming, where the difference between winning and losing a gold medal is measured in hundredths of a second, this drag is very important. A shaved body has less resistance than a hairy one, so the shaved swimmer will move faster.

In 2000, the Speedo Fast Skin suit was introduced to the world. It is based on the fact that water will actually flow better over some rough surfaces than over some smooth surfaces. A shark's skin is quite rough, but it is rough in a very particular way. Sharkskin has ridges that look like a series of stripes. These ridges cause water to circulate in a particular way, which results in less drag in the water. The Fast Skin suit uses a similar design with vertical stripes that channel water flow in a way that creates less drag. These channels actually trap a layer of water next to the suit so that as water flows around the swimmer it rubs against water rather than the suit. Scientific tests on the suit have shown that it can reduce drag by as much as 10 percent in some swimming strokes. This could corre-spond to as much as a 3 to 5 percent increase in speed.

6 Jumping, Climbing, Frisbee, and More

Other Fun Sports

Many sports don't involve balls, or wheels, or water. For some, such as skydiving, athletes need a lot of special training and equipment. For others, such as Frisbee, you just need a flying disk and a friend or two. But in all sports, from the complex to the very simple, some science comes into play. Read on to find out how air resistance, gravity, Bernoulli's principle, simple machines, and other scientific principles affect how some sports work.

Project 1
SKYDIVING

As you have seen in previous activities, in many sports athletes try to decrease the effect of the resistance of air on their bodies and equipment so that they can go faster. But in some sports, such as skydiving, athletes want *more* air resistance. Try this activity to learn more about the uses of air resistance.

Materials

balcony or other place at least 3 yards (3 m) off the ground
timing device   plastic garbage bag
small plastic figure   string
paper   tape
pencil   helper
scissors

Procedure

1. Stand on the balcony with your helper standing below you on the ground. The helper should have the timing device.

2. Hold the small plastic figure off the balcony and release it. Have your helper time how long it takes the figure to fall to the ground. Record the time.

3. Cut a 12-by-12-inch (30-by-30-cm) square from the plastic.

4. Cut 4 pieces of string, each 12 inches (30 cm) long.

5. Tape one end of each piece of string to each corner of the plastic square.

6. Bring the other ends of the strings together and tape them to the plastic figure.

7. Again stand on the balcony with your helper standing below you on the ground.

8. Hold the plastic square near the center so that the figure, attached to the strings, is hanging below the square. Make sure the strings aren't tangled. Release the plastic and have your helper time how long it takes the figure to fall to the ground this time. Record the time. How does this time compare to the previous time?

More Fun Stuff to Do

Try making other parachutes using different-size plastic or other materials such as cloth. Try using different lengths of string. Can you make a parachute that keeps the figure in the air longer?

Explanation

The plastic figure will quickly fall to the ground by itself. But when you attach the strings and plastic square to it, it will take more time to fall.

What you have made in this activity is a parachute, the most important piece of equipment in skydiving and sport parachuting. A **parachute** is an umbrella-shaped device that slows an object's fall from a great height, such as from an airplane. An object attached to a parachute is affected by two forces: gravity pulling it down and air resistance opposing this movement. **Air resistance** is friction on something moving through air. The pull of gravity is much greater than air resistance, so the air only slows the rate of falling. The larger the parachute, the more air resistance it meets, and the slower it, and the object attached to it, fall.

Without air to resist its motion, any object that falls toward Earth would keep moving faster and faster as it fell. It would **accelerate** (speed up) at a rate of 32 ft/sec^2 (9.8 m/s^2). This means that every second, its speed would increase by 32 ft/sec (9.8 m/s).

As a sky diver falls through the air, air resistance begins to increase until its force is equal to the force of gravity. At this point the law of inertia takes over. The law of inertia says that an object in motion at a constant speed will remain going at that speed unless acted on by an outside force. The sky diver will continue to fall, but because there is no outside force (the forces are equal) he will fall at a constant speed and will no longer speed up. This speed is called **terminal speed.** The terminal speed varies for sky divers from about 95 to 125 mph (150 to 200 km/h). Heavier people have higher terminal speeds than lighter people. Also, if the sky diver spreads out her body so that the air hits her chest, she increases the surface area that the air hits, so there is more air resistance. With the increase in air resistance, the diver's terminal speed decreases, so she will fall more slowly.

When the sky diver opens her parachute, air resistance greatly increases because of the increase in surface area. The terminal speed for a sky diver with his parachute open is 10 to 15 mph (15 to 25 km/h), slow enough for her not to get hurt when she lands.

Project 2
HIGH JUMPING

You may have noticed that high jumpers and pole vaulters bend their bodies when they go over the bar. Is it easier to get over the bar that way or is there something else involved? Try this activity to find out.

Materials

1-by-11-inch (2.5-by-30-cm) piece of cardboard
ruler
pencil
plastic drinking straw
paper plate, 7 inches (17.5 cm) in diameter
scissors

Procedure

1. Use the ruler and pencil to draw lines on the cardboard connecting opposite corners. Where the lines meet is the center of mass for the cardboard.

2. Hold the straw horizontally in front of you in your left hand. This represents a high jump bar.

3. Place the cardboard vertically in your right hand next to the straw. This represents a high jumper.

4. Move the cardboard up then rotate 90 degrees left so that it just passes over the straw. Note where the center of mass for the cardboard is located as it passes over the straw.

5. Use the scissors to cut the paper plate in half.

6. Take one half of the plate and cut a 1-inch-wide (2.5 cm) section around the rim. Keep this rim section and discard the rest.

7. Again hold the straw horizontally in front of you in your left hand.

8. Hold the curved paper section in your right hand with the open part of the curve facing left.

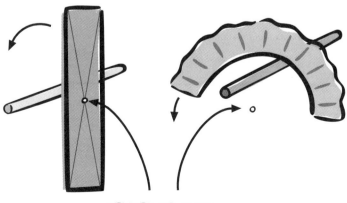

CENTER OF MASS

101

9. Place the curved section next to the straw and move it up until the inside edge of the circle is above the straw, then rotate it so it just passes over the straw. In order to do this, the circle will have to rotate over the straw. As the curved section passes over the straw, picture where the center of mass of the plate would have been. What do you notice?

Explanation

When the cardboard passes over the straw, its center of mass is over the straw. But when the half circle passes over the straw, its center is actually under the straw.

This activity is a good example of how shape can change the location of the center of mass of an object. When you stand upright, your center of mass is located about 1 inch (2.5 cm) below your navel, and midway between your front and back. But when you bend at the waist, your center of gravity is actually located outside of your body! Normally, to get an object over a certain height, you

SPORTS SCIENCE IN ACTION

In the high jump, participants attempt to clear a crossbar by taking off from one foot. Over the past 50 years, jumping styles have changed dramatically. Originally, jumpers used the "scissors" technique and kept their bodies upright over the bar. Later they used the "straddle," in which they approached the bar and kicked their lead leg upward, then contoured their bodies over the bar, facedown. In both of these early techniques, the jumpers' center of mass had to move over the crossbar. But in 1968, high jumping was revolutionized with a technique know as the "Fosbury flop." In the flop, the athlete approaches the bar almost straight on, then twists his body into a reverse curve so that he goes over the bar on his back. The jumper's body can clear the crossbar while his center of mass passes below it, similar to what you saw in this activity. The flop was developed by American Dick Fosbury, who used it to set an Olympic record with a jump of 7 feet 4¼ inches (2.24 m) in Mexico City.

must raise its center of mass above the height. But if the object is curved, it can get over the height while its center of mass is still below the height. So when a high jumper bends to get over the high jump bar, his center of mass is outside his body, and it is possible for his body to clear the bar while his center of mass passes below the bar. Since the center of mass doesn't have to go as high, it takes less effort for the body to go higher when it's curved than it would if it were straight.

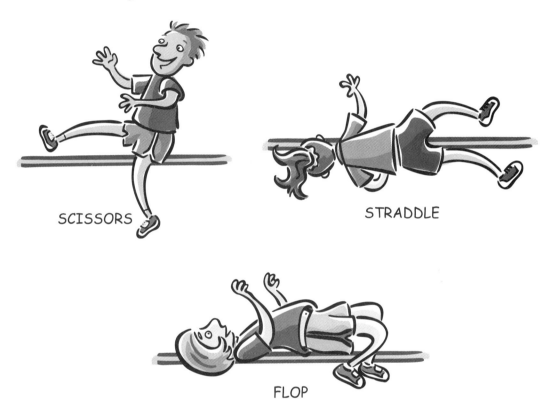

SCISSORS

STRADDLE

FLOP

Project 3
THE FRISBEE

Throwing a Frisbee is fun to do at a park, at the beach, or in your yard. And it's also part of a popular sport called ultimate. (Ultimate is like Frisbee football. One person throws the Frisbee to a partner in the end zone while the other team tries to intercept it.) What makes a Frisbee fly? Take a Frisbee and a friend to the park and do the following experiments.

Materials

Frisbee
friend
large open area, such as a park

Procedure

Part 1: Does the amount of spin have an effect on the flight of the Frisbee?

1. Hold the Frisbee perfectly flat in front of you. Push it forward with no wrist flick. How does it fly?

2. Next, hold the Frisbee flat in front of you. Again throw it, but this time use a quick flick of your wrist. How does it fly this time?

3. Make several other Frisbee throws, increasing the wrist flick to spin the Frisbee more. What happens?

Part 2: Does the angle you hold the Frisbee affect its flight?

1. Hold the Frisbee perfectly flat in front of you. Throw it with a quick flick of your wrist. How does it fly?

2. Next, hold the Frisbee with a slight angle so that its front edge is slightly higher than the edge nearest your body. Again throw it with a quick flick of your wrist. How does it fly this time?

3. Make several other Frisbee throws, increasing the angles of your throw. Can you make the Frisbee come back to you?

More Fun Stuff to Do

Try throwing the Frisbee with the right edge higher than the left edge. What happens to the flight of the Frisbee? What happens when the left edge is higher than the right?

Explanation

The Frisbee will fly better with spin and the front edge slightly higher than the rear edge. If the front edge is a lot higher, the Frisbee will first fly away from you, then return. In the More Fun Stuff to Do activity, if the right edge is higher than the left, the Frisbee will curve left, while if the left edge is higher than the right, the Frisbee will curve to the right.

There is a real lack of research into why the Frisbee flies, although some scientists will take a guess. "The best way to describe it is a combination airplane wing and gyroscope," says one. "If you try to say any more than that, it gets real complicated."

What keeps a Frisbee aloft is probably its platelike shape and its ability to fly forward with its front end tipped up at a slight "angle of attack." Any flat object moving this way will deflect air toward the ground. When the air is forced down, an equal and opposite force is exerted on the disk, and the Frisbee gets some lift. Bernoulli's principle comes into play as well. As the air moving over the top of the Frisbee increases in speed, it creates an area of lower pressure and thus lift.

The spin you give the Frisbee creates a **gyroscopic effect.** As you have seen in previous activities, a rotating object, whether a football, baseball, or bicycle wheel, has a strong tendency to maintain its orientation in space. The faster it spins, the more it wants to hold its position. Thus the spinning Frisbee will maintain a more stable flight than a Frisbee thrown with no spin.

SPORTS SCIENCE IN ACTION

In the 1950s, Fred Morrison, a California building inspector and part-time inventor, developed the "Pluto Platter," the forerunner of the Frisbee. Although the disks appeared to fly, he told prospective customers that they actually rode on an invisible wire. He demonstrated the miracle at county fairs and sidewalk sales, offering the invisible wire for a penny a foot and throwing in a free Pluto Platter with every 100-foot "wire" purchase.

In 1957, the Wham-O Toy Company bought Morrison's invention, altered the design a few years later, and renamed it Frisbee, after the Frisbee Pie Company of Bridgeport, Connecticut. Legend has it that Frisbee pie tins were the original flying disks, used by students at nearby Yale University.

When two students from the Massachusetts Institute of Technology began a study of the Frisbee in 1965, they asked Wham-O about the engineering that went into the development of the Frisbee. They were told, "There isn't any. But if you can figure out why the thing flies, let us know."

Project 4
CLIMBING HIGH

One of the fastest growing sports is rock climbing. In rock climbing climbers move up a steep face of rock using ropes to keep from falling if they lose their grip. Try this activity to learn more about how rock climbers use their ropes.

Materials

1 yard (1 m) of heavy string   broom
small bucket   2 chairs
several rocks or other heavy objects

Procedure

1. Tie one end of the string to the handle of the bucket. Place the rocks in the bucket.

2. Pull the string and lift the bucket. Note the force you exert to lift the bucket.

3. Place the broom handle between two chairs.

4. Place the bucket below the broom handle. Thread the other end of the string over the broom handle.

5. Pull down on the free end of the string to lift the bucket. Again note the force you exert.

6. This time wind the string around the broom handle once. The free end of the string should again hang down.

7. Pull down on the free end of the string to lift the bucket. How much force does this task take?

Explanation

You should have to exert a similar force both to lift the bucket straight up and to lift it using the string running over the broom handle. When you wrap the string once around the handle, however, you will have to exert more force to lift the bucket.

This activity shows how a pulley system and friction are involved in rock climbing. A **pulley** is a simple machine that can be used to change the amount or direction of a pulling force. A pulley is made from a rope or cable that is looped around a support, often a wheel. Friction is a force that stops objects from sliding over each other.

When you lifted the bucket by pulling down on the string hung over the broom, the broom handle acted like a pulley to change the direction of the force. You lifted the bucket by pulling down, which allows you to use gravity to help you lift the bucket. But this kind of pulley doesn't change the amount of force needed to lift the object. When you wrapped the string once around the broom handle before pulling on the end, you created more friction between the string and broom handle. This means that a larger force was needed to lift the bucket.

Rock climbers use rocks that stick out from the rock face, cracks in the rock, grooves where two rocks meet, and corners where the rock face changes direction as handholds and footholds to get to the top. Ropes are used to attach one climber to another and serve as a precaution should one climber fall. In top roping (the safest method), climbers tie webbing to an immovable object at the top of the rock—usually a tree or rock. They attach the webbing to a carabiner, an aluminum alloy ring with a snap-link gate that permits the insertion of the climbing rope. The climbers then pass their climbing rope through the carabiner so that the two ends of the rope dangle down the side of the rock. One end is tied to the climber. The other end is tied to, and held by, a person at the bottom who keeps the rope taut to stop a fall. If the rope is wrapped once around the carabiner (similar to what you did in this activity), the person at the bottom has to exert less force to hold the person in place, due to the friction between the rope and carabiner, should the climber fall.

Project 5
CLIMBING TO THE TOP

Mountain climbers who go up to very high altitudes, such as at the top of Mount Everest, the tallest mountain in the world, need to carry oxygen tanks with them to help them breathe. To see why, try the next activity.

Materials

plastic drinking straw
scissors

Procedure

1. Breathe normally for a few minutes and pay attention to how it feels.

2. Use the scissors to cut a 4-inch (10-cm) piece from the plastic drinking straw.

3. Stick the straw between your lips and breathe in and out through the straw. Do not breathe through your

nose or your mouth. Breath only through the plastic straw. How is your breathing different when you breathe only through the straw?

Explanation

When you try to breathe through the straw, you will find it hard to get enough oxygen. Breathing through a plastic drinking straw simulates what it is like for mountain climbers to breathe at high altitudes. The amount of oxygen that is in the air decreases with altitude, so there is only about two-thirds of the oxygen when climbers are about 18,000 feet (5,500 m) as there is at sea level. When a climber nears the top of Mount Everest at 29,028 feet (8,848 m) above sea level, the air will contain only one-third of the oxygen that air at sea level contains. When there is not enough oxygen in the air, the climber will first become light-headed and dizzy and will generally feel weak. Over time, the body will react to this decrease in oxygen by producing more red blood cells, the part of the blood that carries oxygen. With more red blood cells, the body becomes more efficient at transporting the oxygen to the body cells, and the climber can perform much better.

SPORTS SCIENCE IN ACTION

Attempts to climb Mount Everest began in the early 1920s, and several expeditions came within 1,000 feet (300 m) of the top. But climbers didn't reach the summit until after the development of compressed oxygen bottles, which helped them cope with the low oxygen at high altitudes, and other special equipment to combat Everest's high winds and extreme cold. On May 29, 1953, Edmund Hillary of New Zealand and Tenzing Norgay, a Nepalese Sherpa tribesman, became the first people to reach the top. Since then Everest has been conquered many times and in recent years has even been climbed without the aid of extra oxygen bottles.

SWEET SPOT

In chapter 2, you learned about the balls that are used in sports. But what about the equipment that's used to hit the balls? Have you ever noticed that when you hit a tennis ball with a tennis racket or a baseball with a bat or a golf ball with a golf club the results can really vary? Sometimes the ball seems not to travel very far, while other hits send the ball off like a rocket. How well you hit the ball has to do with where the ball made contact with the racket, bat, or club. The best place is called the sweet spot. Try this activity to find the sweet spot in a tennis racket.

Materials

tennis racket
tennis ball

Procedure

1. Hold the tennis racket so that the handle points upward and the faces of the racket point to your left and right.

2. Hold the tennis racket handle between the thumb and index finger of one hand so that it can swing freely back and forth in front of you.

3. Hold the tennis ball in your other hand.

4. Tap the tennis ball on the face of the tennis racket. What does the tap sound like and how does the tap feel in the hand that is holding the racket? How far does the tennis racket bounce when hit?

5. Tap with the same force in various places on the tennis racket face. Tap around the edges and near the center of the racket. Does the racket move the same amount when hit in each place? Does each hit sound the same? Does each hit feel the same in the hand that is holding the racket?

More Fun Stuff to Do

Try this same activity with a baseball bat and baseball or with a golf club and golf ball. Do you get similar results? Can you find the sweet spot for each?

Explanation

When you hit the tennis racket with the ball, the ball and racket will make a slight noise and the racket will move away from the ball. You will also feel some vibrations in the hand that is holding the racket. As you hit other places on the racket, you will find that hits along the edges of the racket produce more vibrations and less movement of the racket away from the ball. If you hit near the center of the racket, there will be less vibration and the racket will move slightly farther from the ball.

When you hit a tennis ball near the center of the racket, you hit the ball with what is called the sweet spot of the racket. The sweet spot has to do with vibrations in the racket. No matter where a tennis ball hits on a racket, the impact causes the racket to vibrate.

SIDE VIEW

SIDE VIEW

Vibration Node "Sweet Spot"

Fundamental Vibration

First Harmonic of Vibration

There are two kinds of vibrations that can occur. The most obvious is called the fundamental node, where the end of the racket vibrates back and forth. In the other kind of vibration, called the first harmonic, the end of the racket vibrates, but there is also a place in the racket, called a vibration node, where no vibration occurs.

When a tennis ball hits the racket anywhere on the strings, the impact will trigger both the fundamental and harmonic vibrations, and the player will feel the vibration in her hand. However, if the ball strikes the racket in the vibration node, or sweet spot, the first harmonic will not be generated. This is felt by the player as less vibration in her hand. Also, since less energy is lost to a vibrating racket, more energy is transferred into the ball, so the ball moves both faster and farther.

Similar vibrations patterns occur in baseball bats and golf clubs so that when the vibration node or sweet spot is hit in each, less vibration is felt and the ball goes faster and farther.

SPORTS SCIENCE IN ACTION

Companies that make sports equipment want to make tennis rackets, baseball bats, and golf clubs that have larger sweet spots. With a larger sweet spot, beginning players have a greater chance of hitting a good shot. Oversize tennis rackets, aluminum baseball bats, and jumbo golf clubs all have larger sweet spots, which makes it easier to get a good hit.

Project 7
THE CHOP

Have you ever seen a karate expert break boards, bricks, or even blocks of ice with a single blow? Believe it or not, it's not just strength that causes the object to break. It's the science involved in the karate expert's technique that keeps him from breaking his hands. To learn more, try this activity. (But, please, don't try breaking any board or concrete blocks!)

Materials

safety glasses or goggles

$\frac{1}{4}$-by-1-inch-by-2-feet (.3-by-2.5-cm-by-60-cm) pine stick. (This can be purchased at any lumber store.)

sheet of newspaper

Procedure

1. Put on your safety glasses or goggles.

2. Place the stick on the table so that about 6 inches (15 cm) extend over the edge of the table.

3. Lay the sheet of newspaper over the stick, as shown, with the stick centered under the newspaper. Flatten out the newspaper so that there is no air between it and the table.

4. Using the edge of your palm, hit the protruding end of the stick. What happens?

Explanation

When you hit the stick with the newspaper on it, the stick breaks.

When you flatten out the newspaper, you push almost all the air out from under it. However, the large amount of air above the newspaper pushes down on the paper with a great force called air pressure. Air pressure on a normal day is about 15 pounds per square inch (101 kPa). When you hit the stick, the stick breaks because the

force of the air pressure above the newspaper is greater than the force of your hand as you hit the stick.

According to legend, a monk traveled from his home in India to the Shaolin monastery in the Hunan province of China to bring the teachings of a new religion called Zen Buddhism. When he arrived, he found that the monks there were so weak from their inactive life that they would fall asleep during meditations. So the young monk taught them a series of special exercises to make them healthy and strong. These special exercises became the foundation for a method of fighting called kung fu. In A.D. 1379, China and Japan developed an exchange program that brought kung fu to Japan. In 1669, Japan banned weapons. But the people of the Okinawa area needed a way to protect themselves from outlaws and bandits so they combined kung fu with a native martial art called *tode* into what is now known as karate. *Karate* means "open hand" in Japanese and reflects the way the hand is held during a hit.

SPORTS SCIENCE IN ACTION

In karate, karate experts use force to break boards much larger than the stick you broke in this activity. If they punch the board correctly it will break easily, but if they punch it incorrectly they might break bones in their hands. The secret to karate, according to scientists, is the speed and exceptional focus of the strike. A beginning karate student can throw a karate chop at about 20 feet per second (6 m/s), just enough to break a 1-inch (2.5-cm) pine board. But a black belt karate expert can throw the same chop at 46 feet per second (14 m/s). At that speed, a 1.5-pound hand (.68 kg) can deliver up to 2,800 newtons of force. It takes only 1,900 newtons to split a concrete slab 1.5 inches (3.75 cm) thick.

Glossary

accelerate—speed up.

aerodynamics—the study of the forces exerted by air and other gases in motion.

air resistance—friction on something moving through air.

amplitude—the distance from the middle of a wave to its crest.

angle of incidence—the anglex that a ball makes when it strikes a board.

angle of reflection—the angle a ball makes after it bounces off a board.

Archimedes' principle—a principle of science that states that objects that are placed in water are buoyed up by a force equal to the weight of the water it displaces.

break—when the crest of the wave begins to fall forward.

Bernoulli's principle—a principle of science stating that as air moves faster it will produce a lower air pressure.

buoyancy—the upward force that water creates on an object to counter the force of gravity pulling the object down.

catamaran—a two-hulled boat.

center of gravity—the point of an object where the effect of gravity on the object seems to be concentrated.

consolidation time—the time needed for your brain to store information in a more permanent way about how to do a new task.

crest—the highest point of a wave.

elastic collision—a collision where both momentum as well as kinetic energy are conserved.

elastic energy—the energy stored in an object when its shape is changed by stretching (pulling apart) or compressing (pushing together).

electrochemical impulse—the way nerves communicate that uses chemicals to send an electrical signal.

force—a push or pull.

friction—the resistance to motion between two objects that rub against each other.

gear—a toothed wheel.

gravitational potential energy—the energy in an object because of its position and the force of Earth's gravity.

gravity—the attraction between two objects due to their mass. It is also the force that pulls all objects toward Earth.

gyroscopic effect—a strong tendency of a spinning object to maintain its orientation in space.

hypothesis—an educated guess about the results of an experiment you are going to perform.

impulse—when a force is put on an object for a length of time.

keel—the board that protrudes straight down beneath the hull of a sailboat.

kinetic energy—the energy of motion.

law of angular momentum—a law in science that says that a rotating object will stay rotating in that same way unless acted on by an outside force.

law of conservation of momentum—a law in science that says that the momentum of an object, such as a ball, before hitting a board (or colliding with any other object), will be the same after it hits.

machine—any device that helps people do work (or participate in sports) more easily.

momentum—a quantity of a moving object, such as a rolling ball, that is equal to its mass times its speed.

motor cortex—the area of the brain responsible for creating and sending the messages that cause movement.

motor nerves—nerves in the body that direct your muscles to move.

nerves—special cells that communicate using electrochemical impulses.

parachute—an umbrella-shaped device that slows an object's fall from a great height.

pressure—the amount of force divided by the area of the force.

pulley—a simple machine that can be used to change the amount or direction of a pulling force. A pulley is made from a rope or cable that is looped around a support, often a wheel.

pumping—a process where you are raising the center of mass to increase your speed in a skateboard in a half-tube.

Pythagorean theorem—a theorem in mathematics stating that in a right triangle, the square of the triangle's hypotenuse (the longest side of the triangle) is equal to the sum of the squares of the other two sides.

reaction time—the amount of time it takes for a message to travel from the brain to the muscles in the body and cause a movement.

scientific method—a process used to investigate a problem. Involves making a hypothesis, testing it with an experiment, analyzing the results, and drawing a conclusion.

scuba—an acronym for Self-Contained Underwater Breathing Apparatus.

sensory nerves—nerves in the body that collect information from your environment such as hot, cold, touch, pressure, and pain. They send this information to your brain, which decides how to react.

surface tension—the force of attraction among water molecules that creates a "thin skin" on the surface of the water.

tacking—when a sailboat sails into the wind.

terminal speed—the speed at which a sky diver will continue to fall, but because there is no additional outside force (the forces of air resistance and gravity are equal) he will fall at a constant speed and will no longer speed up.

thermal energy—heat energy.

transverse wave—a wave that moves perpendicular to its source.

trough—the lowest point of a wave.

vortices—an area of spinning air.

wavelength—the distance between wave crests.

Index

Sosa, Sammy, 39
speed
  of balls, 20, 24
  of boats, 85–87
  of curveball, 26
  of falling objects, 100
  of Frisbee, 105, 106
  gears and, 62–67
  gravity and, 21–22, 53
  momentum and, 43–44
  in spins, 50–51
  in surfing, 82
  in swimming, 93–95
  of tennis balls, 41
  terminal, 100, 118
  in Tour de France, 67–70
Speedo, 95
speed skating, 57
spin
  of curveball, 26, 28, 31
  of Frisbee, 104, 105–6
  in ice-skating, 49–51
  momentum and, 46
  in skateboarding, 73
  stable, 27–28
spiral, 28
stable base, 57–59
Stalefish, 73
Stars & Stripes (sailboat), 87
surface tension, 79, 87, 118
surfing, 56, 78–82
sweet spot, 111–13
swells, 81, 82
swimming, 93–95
swing, 73

tacking, 89, 118
telemark landing, 54

tennis
  ball, 37–38, 39, 40–42
  reaction time in, 6
  sweet spot in, 111–13
  throwing balls, 20–22
  topspin and, 26, 41
thermal energy, 39, 118
tobagganing, 46
tode, 115
topspin, 26, 41
Tour de France, 67
transverse wave, 81, 118
trough, 81, 118

ultimate, 103
USGA (United States Golf
    Association), 31, 39

velocity. *See* speed
vibrations, 112–13
visualization, 12–13
vortices, 69–70, 118

water balloons, 34–36
water pressure, 91–92
water-skiers, 56, 78–79
wavelength, 81, 118
waves, 80–82
waxing, 54–56
Wham-O Toy Company, 106
wheels, 62–65, 70–72
Wiffle ball, 28, 29, 30
wind, 81, 87, 88–90
Woods, Tiger, 31

Yale University, 106

Zen, 115